CARIBBEAN
potluck

Suzanne & Michelle Rousseau are the official culinary hostesses for the Jamaica Tourist Board, for which they've filmed the 'Island Potluck' web series. Former restaurateurs and award-winning caterers who have thrown parties for the Prime Minister of Jamaica, the Prince of Wales and celebrities like Ewan MacGregor, the sisters are currently filming the first season of their cooking show, 'Two Sisters and a Meal'. Presently residing in Kingston, Jamaica, both girls have lived and travelled widely in the Caribbean, North America, Europe and Asia. To view their recipes, videos and blogs, visit them at www.2sistersandameal.com.

SUZANNE & MICHELLE ROUSSEAU

CARIBBEAN
potluck

MODERN RECIPES FROM OUR FAMILY KITCHEN

Photography by Ellen Silverman

Kyle Books

Dedication

To the legacy of our family

For our grandparents, Hugh and Mae, Hopi and Enid, whose bright spirits have guided us from beyond during the writing of this book

For our parents, Peter and Beverly, for ALWAYS allowing us to be ourselves, and being our champions through success and failure

Published in 2014 by Kyle Books

192–198 Vauxhall Bridge Road
London SW1V 1DX

general.enquiries@kylebooks.com
www.kylebooks.com

ISBN: 978-0-85783-231-3

10 9 8 7 6 5 4 3 2 1

Text © 2014 by Suzanne Rousseau and Michelle Rousseau
Photography © 2014 by Ellen Silverman
Book design © 2014 by Kyle Cathie Ltd

Project editor Anja Schmidt
Designer Lucy Parissi
Photographer Ellen Silverman
Food styling Christine Albano
Prop styling Marina Malchin
Copy editor Sarah Scheffel
Proofreader Liana Krissoff
Production by Nic Jones, Gemma John and Lisa Pinnell

A Cataloguing in Publication record for this title is available from the British Library

Colour reproduction by ALTA, London
Printed and bound in China by C&C Offset Printing Company Ltd.

CONTENTS

FOREWORD

Food is love, nurturing, intimacy, joy and communication; it tells a tale of family, history, culture and tradition.

When Suzanne and Michelle asked me to write the foreword for this first of what I predict to be many publications, I was honoured. This is more than just a cookbook. In this work, Suzanne and Michelle draw on their background and Caribbean upbringing to create a potpourri of delectable, exquisite and tantalising modern Caribbean stories.

As the three of us sat on my patio on a balmy summer August evening in Kingston, Jamaica, these two beautiful and interesting sisters, with very different personalities, briefly shared their lives' journeys, the stories of their travels (all of which encompass food) and the integral part that Caribbean cuisine and culture has played throughout the course of their career and lives. This first publication, *Caribbean Potluck*, flows naturally from the varied menu of their talents and love for the Caribbean region.

In *Caribbean Potluck*, I sense the complementary charge of sister souls who invite us into their world to savour the exquisite flavour of their unique blend of 'Caribbean-ness'. Their food and the recipes they present in this book are the perfect combination of Suzanne's succulent and vibrant emotions and Michelle's smooth and delicate sensitivity.

They bring to the table the merging of two unpretentious souls who have come together to fulfil a legacy, create a new path and serve up some delightful recipes on a platter of love.

'Suzie Q' and 'Michy Boo', as they are affectionately called by friends and family, are exciting, witty and beautiful daughters of the Caribbean; in this cookbook they invite us to experience, through their own personal stories and those of their ancestors, the beauty and mystery of Caribbean history and culture. I have had the privilege of sharing many a food experience with them, so I am particularly delighted by their writings and find myself inspired by their unforgettable journey, even as I drool over their unique culinary creations.

In *Caribbean Potluck*, Suzanne and Michelle share an authentic Caribbean narrative peppered with mouthwatering and exciting recipes. This is not a work to be consumed hurriedly, but instead it should be leisurely imbibed, savoured and relished in a truly spiritual manner, in the manner that one would break bread around a table surrounded by family friends and loved ones.

One Love.
Pat Ramsay

TWO SISTERS:
A JAMAICAN FAMILY STORY

We are sisters with very different personalities; we are friends, we are island girls and we are business partners. Food has been central to both our personal and professional journeys. We never planned to be in the food business – we got here by chance, or perhaps by luck or perhaps by destiny.

We are flip sides to the same coin, and people always marvel at our 'twin' energy, although we are not actually twins. Suzanne is older, but often thought to be younger because of her louder, more outspoken and light-hearted disposition. Michelle is the baby, but is considered the more serious one – the fringe dweller, the observer – which is not always an accurate perception of Suzie's quirky little sister. When we meet people for the first time, we are often told that we, 'Michy Boo' and 'Suzie Q', can be quite an outrageous pair – like 'balls of fire'. We don't know if this is true, but we do know that we get very excited about the people, places and food that we love, and we don't hesitate to share our excitement with anyone willing to listen.

We have many passions in common and take great delight in each other's company: laughing frequently, dancing any chance we get, travelling the world, meeting fabulous people and waxing poetic about books, movies, art and food. We share the belief that life should be celebrated in every moment to its fullest. We love Jamaica and we love the Caribbean way of life; it is an integral part of who we are. We have always believed in promoting the best of Caribbean living, in spite of the many challenges faced by what many consider a 'Third World lifestyle'. We consider being born and raised in Jamaica to be one of our greatest gifts; Jamaica is the blood in our veins, the air that we breathe – the heart and soul of who we are.

Our Modern Caribbean Cooking

Traditional Caribbean food is often represented as hearty, heavy, spicy meals; to an extent, that is true. There are many one-pot dishes and stews that require hours of simmering on the hob to tenderise the inexpensive protein that, historically, was often the only kind locally available. Examples of these traditional one-pot dishes are oxtail and broad beans, curry goat and stew peas in Jamaica,

pepperpot in Guyana, oil down in Grenada and corn soup and pelau in Trinidad. The food we introduce in this book is not limited to traditional dishes – although we do share our contemporary takes on many island classics. During our years operating restaurants and a catering business (and our travels), we have developed a more modern approach to Caribbean food. Although we are from Jamaica, we call the food we cook Caribbean, as our cooking is influenced by all the Caribbean islands – Trinidad and Tobago, in particular, as we spent four formative years there as children.

The recipes we present in this book are our original creations. Some are truly traditional, some are modern versions of traditional dishes and some would not be considered traditionally Caribbean at all; we do consider them Caribbean, however, because of our predominant use of Caribbean ingredients, spices and seasonings. Many of the recipes herein were created and served during our years as the proprietors and chefs at Café Bella, Ciao Bella Caterers and Bellefield Great House. We love Mediterranean cooking, and, in many of our menus, we regularly fuse dishes and techniques from the Mediterranean region with typical Caribbean flavours and seasonings. You'll see examples of Caribbean twists on Italian favourites throughout this book.

The essence of our style, which we call Modern Caribbean Cooking, can be broken down into a few basic concepts:

Marinating Meat: Most Caribbean cooks marinate their meats to add flavour and tenderise the meat. We do the same, no matter what cooking technique we are utilising.

Blending and Balancing Meals: We like to serve a unique blend of savoury and sweet at every meal, with a healthy balance of protein, starch and vegetables, and a wide variety of sides as a way of creating layers of flavour and texture in every meal.

Relying on Caribbean Staples: Ingredients like yam, cassava, cornmeal, sweet potatoes, green and ripe plantain, dasheen (taro), green banana, tropical fruits and fresh coconut feature heavily in our recipes, as these are common staples found in almost any Caribbean kitchen.

Enhancing Food with Caribbean Condiments: We often use a variety of salsas, chutneys, pepper sauces and other condiments to enhance the island flavour of a meal or a dish.

Taking Advantage of Caribbean Sweeteners (and Rum): Common to all the islands, and prevalent in our recipes, is the use of rum, brown sugar, molasses, honey and other sugar cane derivatives in our cooking, baking and beverages. These sweeteners are an inheritance from our past as sugar-producing islands; a nod to our collective past, they also provide flavour and are healthier than the hyper-refined white sugar that's become so prevalent around the world.

You can choose to follow our recipes exactly as we share them, or feel free to make alterations or eliminations based on your palate. Hot pepper is a signature of the cuisine of many of the islands, particularly Jamaica and Trinidad, and we tend to use Scotch bonnet chillies liberally for flavour and spice in many of the recipes in this book. If you are not a chilli lover, feel free to omit these when you try a recipe. We are advocates of invention and creativity, and believe that there are many ways to cook a great dish – the important thing is that you have a good time doing it. This book is a celebration of our cultural heritage and the Caribbean food, flavours and dishes that have influenced our palates and our culinary style over a lifetime.

Caribbean History: Mixing Food and Identity

It is almost impossible to tell a concise, chronological history of the Caribbean as one entity, as it is comprised of such a wide range of territories – each with its own unique historical, social, cultural, racial and political structure that was heavily influenced by the world power that colonised it. And keep in mind that the islands of the Caribbean Sea are not the only territories that make up the Caribbean; the mainland territories of Belize, Suriname, Guyana and French Guiana also form part of the region.

One effective way to celebrate Caribbean identity is through our cuisine, which is influenced not only by our cultural history and our geography but also by the subtle nuances, complexities and paradoxes that make up daily Caribbean life. In essence – no matter where we come from, or what language we speak – we are far more alike than we are different. Our common identity lies in our oral histories; in childhood experiences and memories; in music, dances, attitudes; in our shared zest for life; and, most importantly, in the food: where we eat, how we eat and what we eat.

Throughout the centuries, the Caribbean's warm and welcoming islands have embraced many cultures and races, adopting and adapting the traditions, cuisines and cultural norms of their new residents. From as early as the late fifteenth century, Caribbean food became, and continues to be, an intriguing fusion of different flavours and ingredients inherited from slavery, and from the many migrants who settled in our region over the past five centuries. In the Caribbean of today, we eat many different types of food. While some of these are not indigenous to our region, we always manage to tweak them to suit our palates and lifestyle – and somehow make them ours.

'Our' Foods

As we delved deeper and deeper into the business of cooking and serving Caribbean food, we discovered that what we had always considered to be 'our' foods were not really 'ours' after all, but instead belonged to all peoples of the region. We discovered that the way we prepared our foods – and in particular the 'what', 'where', 'when' and 'how' we consumed them – was, in fact, no different from the way this is done in many other islands in the region. This speaks to both the commonality and the diversity of the Caribbean experience, and validates the existence of a universal culture that is uniquely Caribbean in its essence. Growing up in the Caribbean was quite a treat; we have never forgotten the joys of a childhood well lived. 'Caribbean-ness' dwells in our memories. The daily lilt of voices raised in song, prayer or protest; the perpetual search for the perfect mango that occupied long and lazy summer days; that sweltering summer heat broken only occasionally by the cool Caribbean Sea breeze; the farm animals, goats and cows that roamed the city streets and often found their way into our backyard; young children in school uniforms, agitating neighbourhood dogs; old ladies dressed in their Sunday best under the blazing midday sun en route to church; roadside food, hot and dubious; the pulsing sound of music blasting from cars. This is the rhythm of the Caribbean that dwells in our souls, and we invite you to explore that with us and partake in its beauty and complexity.

A True Caribbean 'Mix-up and Blenda'

Our family is the perfect example of what we call 'the mix-up and blenda' (a Jamaican patois expression meaning 'a diverse mixture and blend of things') that is Caribbean history; complete with our own unique blend of African, French, German, Indian, Scottish, Haitian, Cuban and British heritage. The Rousseau side of the family is descendent from one member of the family and his two sons who came to Jamaica in the nineteenth century via Haiti. Our mother's side of the family is more culturally complex. Our maternal grandfather was born in Cuba and came home to Jamaica at age nine; our maternal grandmother was the daughter of a Scottish immigrant.

Our Fondest Childhood Food Memories

Our childhood memories of food are comforting ones, associated with the tastes and smells of the kitchens of those who made up our world: our parents, Peter and Beverly; our beloved grandparents, Manga (Enid), Mama (Mavis) and Gampi (Hugh); and Aunt Winsome, our father's cousin who lived in England and was mother to our favourite playmate, Caroline. Both of our grandmothers were good cooks in their own right, but Manga was the baker and, boy, could she bake! From puddings, to Easter buns, to patties and plantain tarts, she could do it all. We cherish our early childhood memories of Christmastime at her house, making Christmas puddings with her.

Making pudding at Manga's was a big day. Dried fruits that had been soaked in wine and white rum for months were put in a large washbasin with flour, butter, eggs, allspice, vanilla and nutmeg. Then, as we anxiously awaited the first taste, Manga would sit on a chair and mix, or 'rub', the thick batter by hand with a huge wooden spoon. The aroma was mouth-watering as the ingredients were blended together. After what seemed like hours, we would pour the batter into metal cake pans to steam the pudding, finally getting to lick the spoon – the best part of the day.

Our maternal grandmother, whom we called Mama, was quite the opposite of Manga. While Manga was large in stature and personality, Mama was petite and fiery. She never hesitated to remind us that her 'father was a Scotsman' while rolling her RRRRs, not unlike a Scottish brogue. Mama was known for cooking some of our favourite comfort food – the kind we dreamt about during our university years in Canada, especially on the dark, wintry days. One favourite dish is Mama's cornmeal porridge, always seasoned with just the right amounts of nutmeg, vanilla and condensed milk . . . comfort food at its best! All of our holidays at home shared one requirement: lunch at Mama and Gampi's. We sent our requests for macaroni cheese, salt fish and fried plantains long before we landed at Norman Manley International Airport in Kingston, and Mama never failed to deliver the perfect lunch every time.

Trinidad, or 'Trini' to many island people, was home to us from 1977–82. We have a longtime love affair with Trini food, which continues to grow every time we make our annual trek to Carnival and taste something new. Our daily drive from school while living in Trinidad always involved begging Mummy to stop at the corner shop in Maraval for salt prunes (Chinese plums that have been salted and preserved) and pickled pommecythere (June plum, or as the Trinis say it, 'POM-SEE-TAY'). The pommecythere always sat in a jar of vinegar and hot pepper on the counter, just waiting to be eaten. The salt prunes were huge, red and salty. We also loved the red salt prune dust, which you could buy separately – and we often did.

Our food memories of Trinidad are peppered with tastes of *pastelles* at Christmastime, rotis of every kind, doubles and pelau: a one-pot dish of chicken, gungo (pigeon) peas and rice cooked down with coconut milk and seasonings – delish! Trini food is always highly spiced and peppery.

Mango chow was a staple snack for us during mango season. Fortunately, our yard had some good Julie mango trees, so we could make mango chow every single day of the season. A pickle of sorts made with green or 'turn' (not quite ripe) mangos, cut into thin slivers and marinated with sea salt, pepper, vinegar and hot pepper or pepper sauce, mango chow is the kind of dish that can give you 'colic' (Jamaican for upset stomach); but it's also the kind of snack you can't stop eating once you start. We spent many an afternoon picking 'not quite ripe' mangos and

making chow in the kitchen, then eating it out of a big bowl outside in the yard, barefoot and happy.

Over the years, we have spent time in other Caribbean islands, each different in character and food depending on its colonial heritage. All of the islands have unique, delicious dishes, but a few of our favourites include: nutmeg jam in Grenada; flying fish in Barbados; *ti ponche* (rum punch) in St Lucia; griot pork in Haiti; *chicharronnes de pollo* (local street-side chicken) in the Dominican Republic; conch fritters in the Bahamas; and *frijoles* (black beans) in Cuba. Not to be overlooked is the wonderfully fresh seafood prepared on every island. Our favourites include fried fish and festival at Kingston's Hellshire Beach and shark and bake at Maracas Beach in Trinidad.

Along the way, we learnt to embrace and celebrate everything our Jamaican culture has to offer and to treat every new experience as an opportunity to learn and grow; this has surely kept us on our toes! Jamaican people are full of contradictions, flowery language, enthusiastic responses and many preconceived ideas about the world; they can make you laugh and they can drive you mad, and guess what? We love them! Connecting with the people around us – and the stories of their lives, families and experiences – has greatly influenced this book. We hope you enjoy the cultural mêlée of recipes as much as we do!

CARIBBEAN KITCHEN 101

THE CARIBBEAN STORECUPBOARD

DRIED GOODS / GROCERY ITEMS

Coconut Milk, Coconut Flakes/ Shredded and Desiccated Coconut: Coconut milk comes from the grated white meat of a coconut, and is a popular ingredient in Southeast Asia as well as in the Caribbean. You can buy the liquid canned, or the dehydrated unsweetened coconut milk powder in packets. Unsweetened coconut flakes and desiccated coconut are also available in the baking aisle of supermarkets, and moist sweetened shredded coconut (Baker's Angel Flake) is available from online suppliers.

Excelsior Water Crackers: These oven-baked, fat-free crackers are delicious and an absolute must-have. They go well with a simple cup of tea, or as a snack with Solomon Gundy (a Jamaican pickled herring paste), cheese or jam.

Gungo Peas: Originating in eastern India, these dried peas are also known as pigeon peas. A dish of rice and gungo peas (for recipe, see page 142) is common in the Caribbean, usually accompanied by a meat dish. Pigeon peas can also be used in soups, and are split to make dahl.

Hard Dough (Hardo) Bread, Plait Bread, Coco Bread: These traditional island breads are great vehicles for spreads like butter and jam, and are ideal for hearty sandwiches. Stuff a Jamaican patty in the middle and you have a favourite lunch item.

Red Cow Peas, Black Beans, Split Peas: These are beans and peas used to make dishes such as rice and peas, which is a popular element of Sunday dinner. They are especially delicious when simmered in stews, as they absorb the flavours of the seasonings with which they are cooked.

Rice: A wide variety of white and brown rice is used throughout the Caribbean. White rice is a must, however, to accompany a meal of curried goat (for recipe, see page 96), for example.

CANNED / BOTTLED GOODS

Authentic Hot Pepper Sauce (e.g. Matouk's – not Tabasco!): Matouk's and Walkerswood are two fiery brands of hot pepper sauce that allow you to feel the heat build and fill up your entire mouth, leaving your lips on fire. Both brands sell a variety of different heat levels and flavours from which to choose.

Browning: This is a natural food colouring comprised of caramel colour, vegetable concentrates and seasonings. It is used to give foods a rich, brown and irresistible colour but does not have a taste. Used for both savoury and sweet dishes, like oxtail or Christmas pudding, browning is found in most Jamaican kitchens, but we don't use it in the book.

Canned Ackee: The ackee is Jamaica's national fruit – ackee and salt fish is one of our best-known local dishes. Ackee is creamy and buttery with a mild nutty taste. When raw it has a waxy texture, but canned ackee has a more mushy consistency.

Cassareep: This syrup is made by boiling the juice of the bitter cassava root to the consistency of molasses and flavouring it with spices. Cassareep is produced mostly in Guyana and is the main ingredient in traditional pepperpot, a meat stew (for recipe, see page 103). Traditionally, it was also used to preserve meats for extended periods of time.

Guava Jelly or Jam: This delicious paste is made by extracting the juice from guavas and boiling it with sugar and lime juice to produce a paste, or jelly, when it cools. Sweet and tart to the taste buds, guava jelly is amazing with peanut butter, cheese, toast and fresh banana bread.

Honey: Honey is as sweet as granulated sugar, making it a natural sugar alternative. Flavours vary depending on the nectar of the flower being used by the honey bee. If you can get your hands on some Jamaican honey, use it for these recipes. It is darker, more caramelised and sweeter.

Hot Pepper Jelly and Papaya, Banana and Mango Chutneys: An ideal way of preserving fruits, papaya, banana and mango chutneys are spicy-sweet additions to any savoury meal. Pepper jelly is made by combining hot local chillies (usually Scotch bonnet) with sugar to make a spicy jelly that complements cheese, sandwiches and all kinds of meats. Chutneys are made from a wide variety of fruits that are cooked down with vinegar, sugar, seasonings and spices. Jellies and chutneys are often condiments at any Caribbean table.

Marmalade: A preserve made from boiling the juice and peel of citrus fruits (like lemon, lime, mandarin, oranges and grapefruit) with sugar and water, marmalade is distinguished from jam by the peel that is incorporated into the preserve, creating a rougher and chunkier texture and contributing a slightly bitter taste. We love to serve blue cheese with marmalade, a pairing of classic British ingredients that we have adopted in the Caribbean.

Molasses: This is the dark, concentrated liquid by-product of the sugar cane refining process. It used to be the primary sweetener in the Caribbean islands and elsewhere before refined white sugar was developed. Molasses is found in many stouts, and used in the distillation of rum.

Pickapeppa: Sometimes described as the 'Jamaican A-1', Pickapeppa sauce is made from tamarind. It adds sweetness and spice to any meal, and is particularly delicious as an accompaniment to a piping hot Jamaican patty.

DRIED / PICKLED MEATS & SEAFOOD

Salt Beef, Pork, Pig's Tail: An inheritance from our colonial history, when meats of all kinds were salted or cured in order to preserve them for long periods of time without refrigeration, salt beef and pork are still consumed in many of the islands. They add flavour and protein to soups, stews and one-pot dishes like rice and peas or 'oil down', a delicious stew made with coconut milk.

Salt Cod: Also known as salt fish, codfish and *bacalao*, this is cod that has been preserved by drying after salting. It is a staple in the cuisine of almost all Caribbean islands and can be prepared in a number of ways, like in the Trini-Style Salt Fish and Bake on page 151. Salt cod was a part of the Triangular Trade between Europe, Africa and the Americas. High-quality cod was sold in Europe, but traders sold a lower-end product of poorly cured salt fish called 'West India cure' to plantation owners in the Caribbean, who served it as a cheap form of food for the slave population. In exchange, European traders received sugar, molasses, rum, cotton, tobacco and salt.

Other Salted Fish: Like salt fish and salt mackerel, salt herring is commonly consumed in the Caribbean as a breakfast dish where it's sautéed with peppers, onions and tomatoes. It is also often pickled with a combination of vinegar, hot peppers, onions and vegetables, and consumed as a snack on water crackers. Salt mackerel is stewed down in coconut milk with vegetables and seasonings in one of Jamaica's most popular breakfast dishes: mackerel rundown. Served with boiled green bananas, this is one dish that is not to be missed!

ISLAND PRODUCE

In this section, we share an extended glossary of common Caribbean fruits and vegetables, all of which we use in our recipes and some of which may be unfamiliar to you. We provide alternative names, information on how they are used and substitutes for many of these items. This will enable you to identify the ingredients you are buying and provide options for alternatives should any of these items not be available.

Ackee: A native to tropical West Africa, this waxy fruit originally came to Jamaica from West Africa on a slave ship – it is often said that many slaves used to wear the seeds as a talisman around their neck for good luck. If you can't locate fresh ackee, canned ackee is a perfectly acceptable substitution. See page 24 on preparing fresh ackee.

Allspice (Pimento): In Jamaica, we call the allspice berry 'pimento'. It is a prominent flavour in our cuisine that's used in many dishes, either whole or ground, the most famous of which is our infamous spicy jerk, a spice blend/rub used on chicken and other meats. In fact, most of the world's supply of allspice/pimento is grown in Jamaica. The allspice or pimento berry has a unique taste – like a blend of nutmeg, cinnamon, black pepper and clove.

Avocado (Pear / Zaboca): The avocado comes in over 80 varieties. In Jamaica, we call it 'pear', while in Trinidad they refer to it as 'zaboca'. The king of Jamaican avocados, called a Simmons Pear, is very large and has a green skin with a firm and slightly sweet flesh. Jamaican avocados are only available seasonally, and during pear season, slices of avocado presented on platters and sprinkled with sea salt are

a staple at most dinner tables. We also love it on an Excelsior water cracker (see page 15) with pickled herring.

Blue Mountain Coffee: Jamaica is famous the world over for its Blue Mountain coffee, which gets its name from the Blue Mountains where the coffee beans are grown. The coffee industry began in 1725, when Sir Nicholas Lawes, Governor of Jamaica 1718–22, brought seedlings from Martinique and planted them on his estate. Over the last several decades, Blue Mountain coffee has developed a reputation for its excellence, making it one of the most expensive and sought-after coffees in the world.

Callaloo: This leafy, spinach-like vegetable has a distinctively Caribbean origin. Amaranth is the variety of callaloo found in Jamaica. Also referred to as Chinese spinach or Indian kale, amaranth should not be confused with the callaloo found in the eastern Caribbean, which refers to the leaves of the dasheen plant (also known as taro). Some like callaloo soft, while others prefer it crisp; either way, it is often cooked down with onions, garlic, thyme and Scotch bonnet chilli – usually for a hearty breakfast; see page 23 on how to prepare callaloo. Besides spinach, kale and spring greens are good substitutes.

Chadon Beni (Culantro): Most popularly known as chadon beni in the English Caribbean, this is a prominent flavour in the cuisine of Trinidad and Tobago. It is also known as *recaito* in Puerto Rican cuisine. Fresh coriander is similar in flavour, but chadon beni is a much more resinous herb and thus more intense and potent. Coriander may be substituted for chadon beni in any dish. See page 46 for a chadon beni oil.

Cho Cho: A member of the squash family, this rough, prickly-skinned, pear-shaped vegetable grows on vines in cool temperatures. Upon slicing it open, you'll find a very pale green and watery interior, with a soft white seed. Known elsewhere as chayote, mirliton or christophene, cho

cho is probably the most widely used vegetable in the Caribbean; each country has its favourite way to prepare it. Courgette makes a suitable substitute.

Cinnamon: This sweet spice is obtained from the inner bark of trees from the genus Cinnamumum. It is harvested in the rainy season, then dried in curls or ground into powder. In the Caribbean, cinnamon is used to flavour both sweet and savoury foods, but is particularly popular in baking, porridges, drinks and sauces.

Cloves: Native to the Maluku Islands (formerly known as the Moluccas or Spice Islands) in Indonesia, cloves are the aromatic dried flower buds of an evergreen tree. They add a unique flavour to marinades, soups, drinks and pastries, and pair well with cinnamon, allspice, citrus and vanilla.

Coconut: A member of the palm family that's native to Malaysia, the coconut tree yields fruit all year long, which helps explain its prominence in Caribbean cuisine. Coconut is edible in both its green and mature forms.

Both the water and the 'jelly', or meat, of the green coconut find their way into island drinks, and meat from the mature, or dried, coconut adds taste to desserts. Coconut milk (liquid and powdered) is now widely sold everywhere in cans and packets, but in the Caribbean fresh coconut milk is often used in traditional recipes. We provide a recipe on page 24, if you'd like to try it too.

Cocoa or Cacao: The Maya people of the Yucatan Peninsula are known as being the first to domesticate the cocoa plant. Its seeds are used to make cocoa powder and chocolate. Good ole Jamaican chocolate 'tea' is made by grating and boiling fresh cocoa balls with milk or coconut milk, and sweetening the beverage with brown sugar or condensed milk.

Ginger or Ginger Root: This fragrant spice comes from the plant *Zingiber officinale*. Cultivation began in South Asia and has since spread to East Africa and the Caribbean. It is consumed as a delicacy, medicine or spice. Whether added as an a seasoning in a dish, pickled in vinegar or sherry for a snack or steeped for tea, ginger is very useful for both culinary and healing purposes.

Green Banana: Although similar in appearance to yellow bananas, the green banana's flesh is firm and starchy, rather than soft and sweet. A staple starch for many tropical populations, green bananas make great crisps, salads and porridge, or are enjoyed simply boiled. See page 148 on how to prepare green bananas.

June Plum (Pommecythere): A tropical fruit containing a fibrous and spiky stone, this is known by many names in various regions, including pommecythere in Trinidad and Tobago, Dominica, Guadeloupe and Martinique. This versatile fruit can be enjoyed when ripe or juiced. In its unripened state, it is good for making jellies, jams, pickles and sauces. Substitute June plums in our Mango Chow recipe, page 185, if you like.

Limes: Limes are one of the most important ingredients in Jamaican sauces and marinades, and are used to perk up both sweet and savoury dishes. Jamaican limeade, made with brown sugar, is one of the island's most popular drinks and can be found in the fridges of most Jamaican homes. Jamaican limes have a light yellow skin when ripe, though they are often picked green because they go bad rapidly when ripe. You can substitute whatever limes are readily available in your local supermarket or greengrocers.

Mango: A fleshy stone fruit native to South Asia, mango is now distributed worldwide and has become one of the most cultivated fruits in the tropics. There are hundreds of different varieties and many different types in the islands, all with a slightly different flavour profile, texture and skin, but all sweet and juicy. Some examples of the many varieties of mango in Jamaica alone are Julie, East Indian, Bombay, Hayden, Nelson, Sweetie, Blackie and Number 11, to name but a few. You can use whatever mangos you find in your local supermarket or greengrocers in the recipes in this book.

Nutmeg: An evergreen tree indigenous to the Banda Islands of Maluku in Indonesia, the nutmeg tree is important for two spices derived from the fruit: nutmeg and mace. Nutmeg is the roughly egg-shaped seed of the tree. Grenada is one of the largest exporters of nutmeg and, accordingly, it is called the Spice Island of the Caribbean. Nutmeg is used to flavour many foods, desserts and drinks in the islands and is a defining flavour in all kinds of Jamaican porridge. Grenadians make a unique and delicious nutmeg jam that is a must-try.

Ortanique: A cross between a Valencia orange and a tangerine, this citrus fruit was discovered in the parish of Manchester in central Jamaica in the early 1920s. According to Jamaican folklore, it was developed with the help of a pair of lovebirds – one living in an orange tree, the other in a tangerine tree. Extremely sweet but well balanced with acidity, it also has a strong, rich aroma. See our Baked Ham with Ortanique-Ginger Glaze on page 84. Oranges can be used in lieu of ortanique in any recipe.

Papaya (Pawpaw): 'Pawpaw', as Jamaicans call it, is native to the tropics of South America. Orange in colour when ripe with many small seeds, it is mildly sweet when eaten raw, while the green papaya is better in chutney and relishes. Papaya juice is also refreshing; it is often consumed for breakfast topped with a squeeze of fresh lime. See the Ackee Wontons with Papaya Dipping Sauce on page 36.

Passion Fruit: Also known as granadilla, this pleasantly sweet and simultaneously tart fruit is said to have originally come from South America. Two main types, purple and yellow, are widely cultivated in the Caribbean. Inside are sacs with light orange pulpy juice and many small seeds. Passion fruit can be used raw or cooked, as an ingredient in salads, desserts sauces or juices. We also like it in desserts, like the Lemon Passion Fruit Squares on page 172.

Plantain: Technically a banana-family fruit but generally regarded as a starchy vegetable, plantains are inedible raw; cooked plantains are widely served as starters or side dishes. Plantains are used both when green and when ripe, but the ripe plantains are most popular, whether fried, boiled or roasted. The unripe (green) plantain becomes sweeter and less starchy as it ripens, turning yellow. Plantain is eaten widely throughout the entire Caribbean region; each country has its own particular preparation. See page 138 for help to prep green plantains.

Pindars (Peanuts): Known by many local names such as earthnuts, groundnuts and monkey nuts, despite its name and appearance, the peanut is not a nut but rather a legume. In Jamaica, peanuts are freshly roasted by roadside vendors with mobile roasters at traffic lights across the island. They are also eaten raw, added to soups and used to make sweets like peanut brittle and 'pindarcake', sold by locals.

Pineapple: Named after its resemblance to the pine cone, this tropical plant of South America is cultivated from a crown cutting of the fruit, which could flower in 20–24 months and fruits in the following 6 months. Pineapples cannot be picked until ripe because their starch does not convert to sugar after picking. Cowboy and Sugar Loaf are the two most-consumed types of pineapple in Jamaica, but you can use any pineapple found in your local supermarket or greengrocers in our recipes. They can be eaten fresh, cooked in chutneys, salsas or other dishes or as a juice.

Pumpkin: A gourd-like squash with a thick, green or yellow shell, pumpkin is one of the most consumed vegetables in the islands, particularly in Jamaica, as it grows all year around, is nutritious and filling and adds body to soups, rice dishes and stews. The calabaza pumpkin is most similar in texture to Jamaican pumpkin, but any starchy squash can be used, such as butternut.

Scotch Bonnet Chilli: Fiery and ranging in colour from yellow to orange to red, the Scotch bonnet is considered the leading hot pepper in Jamaica, and one of the hottest chillies in the world. They have an incredible flavour and are used to season many types of dishes (as you'll see throughout this book), and are often found in hot sauces and condiments. Paired with allspice, these chillies are the basis for Jamaica's jerk seasoning. The seeds hold the most intense heat and can be saved for cultivation. We mostly deseed these chillies for the recipes in this book but sometimes leave them in for serious heat. Habanero chillies offer a similar level of heat.

Sorrel (Roselle): An annual plant sometimes called *flor de Jamaica*, which originated in West Africa, sorrel produces deep red flowers that are steeped to make a festive drink, also called 'sorrel', popular around the Christmas season and including ginger, cloves, sugar and rum. Sorrel is also used to make chutney and tea.

Sweetsop: Also called custard apple or sugar apple, this fruit is native to the tropical Americas and widely grown in Colombia, El Salvador, India and the Philippines. Protected by a green, rough and bumpy exterior, sweetsop breaks open easily when ripe, revealing its pulpy white segments with many black seeds.

Sugar Cane: A species of tall grass native to the warm and tropical regions of South Asia, sugar cane has stout, jointed, fibrous stalks that are rich in sugar and measure 1.8–6m tall. All Caribbean sugar, molasses and rum come from sugar cane, which can also be eaten raw or processed to make granulated or brown sugar. The Dutch introduced sugar plantation societies using African slave labour to the Caribbean in 1640. By the end of the seventeenth century, Jamaica had become England's main 'Sugar Island' and remained the world's largest sugar exporter until the 1830s, when slavery was abolished and Cuba overtook its neighbour in sugar production.

Sweet Potato: A large, starchy root vegetable, sweet potato is hard when reaped but softens when cooked. Sometimes confusingly referred to as 'yam', the sweet potato is very distinct from a genuine yam (see entry below), which is native to Central Africa and Asia. Its skin colour varies among yellow, orange, brown and purple, while inside can range from light yellow to orange. It is eaten widely throughout the Caribbean – enjoyed roasted, mashed or fried as crisps or fries, and made into a sweet pudding with raisins and spices. See the sweet potato fries on page 55.

Tamarind: The tamarind tree produces fruit in pods that's used in many cuisines around the world. It is fleshy with a sweet and sour taste when eaten straight from the red-brown pod. In the Caribbean, tamarind is used in many savoury dishes, as a pickling agent or to make sauces. A popular snack in the Caribbean is tamarind balls, which are coated in granulated sugar, spices and tamarind juice.

Thyme: A member of the mint family, this herb has a woody stem covered by small, green, aromatic leaves. Best cultivated in a hot, sunny location with well-drained soil, it is used widely in the Caribbean, particularly in Jamaican cuisine. Whenever possible, use fresh thyme rather than dried to capture the superior flavour.

Yellow Yam: Brought to the Caribbean from West Africa as a way to feed slaves working on sugar plantations, yellow yam is one of the most widely consumed ground provisions in the local diet. Although the sweet potato is referred to as a 'yam' in parts of the USA and Canada, it is not of the same family. True yam is a firmer and more starchy root vegetable that is enjoyed barbecued, roasted, fried and boiled. See the recipes on pages 43 and 127.

HOW TO PREP BASIC ISLAND INGREDIENTS

If you're not familiar with some of the island ingredients used in the recipes in this book or are unsure how to prepare them, in this section, we present you with step-by-step descriptions on how to work with some key items. Be sure to check out our online series, 'Caribbean Kitchen 101', where we demonstrate these how-tos. The videos can be accessed through our website: 2sistersandameal.com.

HOW TO WORK WITH A SCOTCH BONNET CHILLI

1 Avoid touching your eyes and face when handling the Scotch bonnet.

2 If you just want to add the chilli's aroma to your soup or stew, simply add the whole Scotch bonnet to the pan, along with the other vegetables. Just be careful not to burst the Scotch bonnet during cooking by mixing too vigorously; when the Scotch bonnet has softened down, be gentle when removing it. If the Scotch bonnet bursts, the seeds will disperse throughout the soup, making it very, very hot.

3 For mild spice, add two to three slices of the Scotch bonnet, seeds removed. Cut the slices from the end without the stalk.

4 To increase the spice, add an additional slice or two of the Scotch bonnet and seeds to taste.

HOW TO CLEAN AND PREP CALLALOO

1 large bunch callaloo yields about 525g cooked

1 Cut the stems off the calalloo leaves and strip the leaves from the stalks, if desired. (You can keep the leaves on the stalk, if you like, but when making a quiche, filling or dip, it is best to strip them off.)

2 Place the leaves in a medium stainless-steel bowl. Add 1 teaspoon sea salt and toss to coat, then rinse the callaloo with cold water to remove any insects. Finely slice. At this point, the callaloo is ready to be sautéed or steamed. Cook until bright green in colour, but don't overcook, as the leaves will turn brown. Note: Callaloo leaves release a lot of water during cooking, so use very moderate amounts of fat to sauté and very little water if steaming.

HOW TO PEEL AND PREP CHO CHO (CHAYOTE)

4 cho cho yield about 1kg cooked cho cho

1 Using a potato peeler, peel the cho cho under running water, as it can have a slimy consistency. Slice in half lengthways and scoop or cut out the core. Raw peeled cho cho can be cut into cubes, chopped or julienned.

2 Sauté in a little oil or toss with olive oil and herbs and roast in an oven for 35 minutes. Like courgettes, cho cho has a high water content and cooks quickly.

HOW TO PEEL AND PREPARE YELLOW YAM

1.3kg raw diced yam yields about 750g cooked

1 Fill a large bowl with fresh water mixed with 1 tablespoon salt. Place it nearby because yellow yam immediately turns black when peeled.

2 First, rinse the yam well under running water to remove any dirt particles.

3 Peel the yam under running water because it is quite slimy and as it oxidises it changes colour quickly. Alternatively, rub 1 teaspoon vegetable oil on your palms before peeling to prevent skin irritation. Immediately place the yam in the bowl of salted water until ready to use.

4 Yam can be boiled and eaten whole, roasted or mashed. Just before you plan to cook it, remove the raw yam from the salted water and cut or slice as the recipe instructs.

5 To boil yam, slice it and bring a deep saucepan of salted water to the boil. Add the yam to the boiling water and cook for about 30 minutes or until tender. Serve warm.

HOW TO PICK AND BOIL ACKEE

1 dozen fresh ackee pods or 4 fresh ackee fruits yield about 240g cooked ackee

1 Choose an ackee fruit with open red skin, as this indicates ripeness. Warning: consuming ackee when the skin is closed can result in severe illness, as certain parts of the ackee are poisonous. Remove the ackee pods by twisting them gently with your fingers from the skin; each ackee should have about three pods. The pods are firm, waxy and yellow, and each has a black seed attached to the top.

2 Remove the seed from each pod by twisting the seed to the right. Using a small knife, remove the red thread-like substance inside the pod and discard; this is the poisonous part. Repeat with the rest of the pods. Leave the pods whole and clean the ackee fruit well under running water.

3 Bring a saucepan of salted water to the boil and add the ackee pods. (We like to season the salted water with a sprig of fresh thyme, but this is optional.) Boil for 15–20 minutes or until the pods become a brighter yellow and soft and buttery in texture but still slightly firm; you don't want to overcook them, as they will become very mushy and difficult to work with.

4 At this point, the ackee is ready to be used in one of our recipes; this is the stage it is in when you buy canned ackee. Use immediately or freeze in a resealable plastic bag for up to 1 week.

HOW TO PICK AND BOIL SALT FISH

450g whole salt cod with skin and bones yields about 250g ready-to-cook salt fish

1 Soak the salt cod in fresh water for about 1 hour.

2 Bring enough fresh water to cover the cod to the boil in a large saucepan over a high heat. Add the cod and boil for about 35 minutes until the flesh of the fish flakes easily when picked. Taste a small piece of the fish, and if it still seems too salty, change the water and boil for another 20 minutes. Drain and transfer the fish to a chopping board.

3 If the fish has bones and skin, scrape the skin from the back of the fish with a knife and discard. Using your fingers, pick through the fish and discard the bones. There are many small bones, so this can be a laborious process, but we are always meticulous about picking out as many as we can. Flake the flesh into medium flakes – make sure the flakes are not too small or crumbly in appearance. (If deboned and skinned salt cod or skin-on salt cod fillets – *bacalao* from Spain or Portugal – are available, simply soak and then boil and flake as described above.) At this point, the fish is ready to be used in a recipe as is or marinated and cooked some more.

HOW TO MAKE FRESH COCONUT MILK

1 whole mature coconut yields 600–700ml coconut milk

1 Crack open the coconut shell with a hammer. Using a small knife, remove the hard coconut meat that is attached to the pieces of shell.

2 Chop or grate the coconut meat and place in a blender. Add 700ml water and purée thoroughly.

3 Strain the liquid through a fine-mesh sieve, pressing down on the remaining pulp with the back of a spoon until all the remaining liquid has been extracted and the pulp is dry. Use the coconut milk immediately or freeze in an airtight container for up to 4 weeks.

FRESH COCONUT WATER

1 fresh coconut yields 600–700ml coconut water

1 Start by picking the coconut that's just for you – do you prefer more water, softer meat or just enough water with a thicker, white meat? Younger, greener coconuts tend to have less water and more of the thick, white 'jelly' you eat after drinking. The water tends to get sweeter as the coconut gets older, identified by a browner outer husk. You can also shake the nut and listen to gauge the amount of liquid inside.

2 Place the coconut firmly on a sturdy chopping surface – preferably outdoors. Hold one end (keeping your fingers clear of the end you'll be chopping!) and, using a sharp machete or large knife, chop away at the husk at the other end until the inner shell is exposed, leaving a large enough hole to drink or pour the water.

3 You can now drink the water straight from the coconut using a straw, or pour coconut water into a container and store in the refrigerator.

4 To get the meat inside, cut the coconut in half along the grain with the machete. Scrape the coconut jelly, or meat, away from the shell using a piece of the husk as a spoon or using an everyday spoon from the kitchen.

FETIN' TIME

LIGHT SOUPS AND SNACKS

Our time living in Trinidad in the 1970s was defined by what the Trinis call *fetin'* and *limin'* (that's Trini speak for partying and socialising). Our parents loved to entertain and our household became known for hosting the sweetest fetes around town. We have many a fond memory of our mother rustling up quick but irresistible eats in the kitchen while our dad served his signature cocktails to the guests. Everyone knew that the *pickins* and *sippins* at our house would be tasty – and always abundant.

Fetin' is a quintessential element of Caribbean living. If you have yet to experience the bacchanal of a Trini soca fete, the raw vibes and pounding bass of a Jamaican street dance or the decadence of a Carnival mass, then we hope that you'll have the chance to visit our islands and join the party soon. No matter what the occasion, the goal is the same – to laugh, eat, drink, dance, sweat and share in the celebration of life with friends and family.

But in the islands, it is common for friends or family to just drop in unannounced for a drink and a last-minute lime, or party. Ultimately, we don't need a reason to entertain – and neither do you. So, in this chapter, we've provided recipes for *pickins* and *sippins* that are all perfect for impromptu parties. Many of these party snacks can be made ahead, while others are quick to throw together. All are guaranteed to keep you and your guests happy.

GOURMET COCKTAIL PATTIES (PASTELITOS)

In the 1930s, our great-grandmother, Martha Mathilda Briggs, was a commercial baker well known across the island for her Jamaican beef patties, Briggs Patties. Ma Briggs was born in Cuba, and the basis for the infamous patty recipe that she brought to Jamaica could have been the pastel. This light Spanish pastry is traditionally filled with *picadillo* – cooked-down beef mince that often includes raisins and olives – and has clear similarities to the modern-day Jamaican beef patty. Here, we share some unique new filling recipes that bring a bit of modern Caribbean flavour to *pastelitos*: a Trini-style chicken with raisins, capers and olives; curried pumpkin; beef chutney; and cheese and creole lobster. If you can't be bothered to prepare fresh pastry, you can use ready-made puff pastry. Filo pastry also makes for an interesting version of these party snacks.

Makes 18–20 (10cm) patties

450g plain flour
1 teaspoon sea salt
225g cold unsalted butter,
cut into 1cm pieces
60ml ice-cold water
filling of choice (recipes follow)
1 medium egg, beaten with 1 tablespoon
water

Method

1 Using a fine-mesh sieve, sift together the flour and the salt into a large bowl. Gently rub the butter into the flour mixture with your fingertips until the mixture achieves a sandy texture. Add the water all at once and mix just until the flour is incorporated and the dough forms a mass. Wrap the dough in clingfilm and chill in the refrigerator overnight. Remove 1 hour before use to let the dough come to room temperature.

2 Prepare your filling of choice. (Alternatively, you can make the filling up to 2 days ahead and refrigerate.)

3 Preheat the oven to 190°C/gas mark 5. Divide the dough into four portions. Roll out each portion 3mm thick and cut into 10cm rounds, creating as little waste as possible. Leftover dough may be tightly wrapped in a freezer bag and frozen for up to 2 weeks.

4 Fill each round of pastry with about 1 tablespoon filling (if you're making Beef Chutney and Cheese Patties, see Note, page 30), then fold the pastry in half and crimp the edges with a fork to seal. Score the top of each pastry and brush with the egg wash. Bake for 30–35 minutes or until the tops are golden brown.

CURRIED PUMPKIN FILLING

Makes 12 patties

1 tablespoon vegetable oil
30g onion, finely chopped
30g spring onion, finely chopped
2 garlic cloves, chopped
1 teaspoon peeled and very finely chopped
fresh ginger
½ Scotch bonnet chilli, deseeded and very
finely chopped
1 tablespoon curry powder or ground
turmeric
230g peeled and deseeded pumpkin, cubed
1 handful fresh coriander leaves, chopped
25g coconut milk powder mixed with 120ml
water or 120ml canned coconut milk
sea salt and freshly ground black pepper

Method

1 Warm the oil in a large sauté pan over a medium heat. Sauté the onion, spring onion, garlic and ginger. When the onions are wilted, stir in the Scotch bonnet and curry powder or turmeric and cook for 2–3 minutes until aromatic.

2 Add the cubed pumpkin and coriander, quickly toss with the onion mixture, then pour in the coconut milk; simmer for 2–3 minutes. Season with salt and pepper. Smash the pumpkin mixture with a potato masher and leave to cool before filling the patties.

TRINI-STYLE CHICKEN FILLING

Makes 12 patties

3 garlic cloves, chopped
1 tablespoon chopped fresh thyme
½ Scotch bonnet chilli, deseeded and very
finely chopped
sea salt and freshly ground black pepper
1 tablespoon olive oil
1 x 225g boneless, skinless chicken breast
2 tablespoons vegetable oil
½ small onion, chopped
¼ red pepper, chopped
1 tomato, deseeded and diced
2 teaspoons tomato purée
1 teaspoon ground paprika
40g raisins
1 tablespoon sliced green olives
2 teaspoons capers, rinsed and drained
1 handful fresh coriander leaves, chopped
1 teaspoon soy sauce

Method

1 Combine 1 teaspoon of the chopped garlic, the thyme, Scotch bonnet, a pinch of salt, a grind of fresh pepper and the olive oil in a baking dish or resealable plastic bag. Add the chicken and then leave to marinate in the fridge for about 2 hours. Remove the chicken breast from the marinade and dice it into very small pieces, then set aside.

2 Warm the vegetable oil in a large sauté pan over a medium heat. Sauté the onion, red pepper, tomato and the remaining garlic. Add the chicken and sauté for 5–8 minutes until cooked through. Add the tomato purée and paprika and cook for about 1 minute, then add the raisins, olives, capers and coriander. Mix well, sprinkle with the soy sauce and mix again until well combined. Leave to cool before filling the patties.

BEEF CHUTNEY AND CHEESE FILLING

Makes 12 patties

4 tablespoons olive oil

3 tablespoons finely chopped onion

3 tablespoons finely chopped spring onion

1 teaspoon chopped garlic,
plus 4 whole cloves, peeled

2 tablespoons chopped fresh thyme,
plus 2 sprigs

2 tablespoons soy sauce, plus 2 teaspoons

175g beef mince

1 tablespoon chopped pepper

½ Scotch bonnet chilli, deseeded and very finely chopped

sea salt and freshly ground black pepper

115g good melting cheese, such as Gruyère or goat's cheese, sliced

65g papaya, banana or mango chutney

Method

1 Combine 2 tablespoons of the oil, 1 tablespoon of the onion, 2 tablespoons of the spring onion, the chopped garlic, chopped thyme and the 2 tablespoons soy sauce in a baking dish or resealable plastic bag. Add the beef mince and then leave to marinate for 15–20 minutes.

2 To make the filling, heat the remaining 2 tablespoons oil in a large frying pan and sauté the whole garlic cloves, the remaining 2 tablespoons onion and 1 tablespoon spring onion, the pepper and Scotch bonnet for 2–3 minutes. Add the beef to the vegetables and sauté for about 5 minutes until browned. Add the sprigs of thyme and 2 teaspoons soy sauce and mix to combine. Season well with salt and pepper. Leave to cool before filling the patties (see Note).

Note: You'll fill each patty with about 1½ tablespoons beef filling, a small piece of cheese and a dab of chutney.

LOBSTER CREOLE FILLING

Makes 12 patties

1½ teaspoons olive oil

1½ garlic cloves, finely chopped

juice of 1 lime (about 1 tablespoon)

sea salt and freshly ground black pepper

1 teaspoon chilli powder

¼ Scotch bonnet chilli, deseeded and finely chopped

1½ teaspoons chopped fresh thyme,
plus 2 sprigs

225g fresh or thawed frozen raw lobster meat, chopped

15g salted butter

½ spring onion, chopped

¼ onion, chopped

2 tablespoons chopped red pepper

1 teaspoon paprika

2 teaspoons tomato purée

60ml white wine

180ml double cream

½ bunch fresh parsley, chopped

25g Parmesan cheese, freshly grated

Method

1 Combine the oil, one-third of the garlic, the lime juice, ½ teaspoon salt, pepper to taste, ½ teaspoon of the chilli powder, the Scotch bonnet and chopped thyme in a baking dish or resealable plastic bag. Add the lobster meat and then leave to marinate in the fridge for about 1 hour.

2 Melt the butter in a large frying pan. Add the spring onion, onion, red pepper, sprigs of thyme and the remaining two-thirds of the garlic and sauté for 2–3 minutes until wilted. Add the lobster, paprika and remaining ½ teaspoon chilli powder and season with salt and pepper. Sauté, stirring frequently, for about 3 minutes until the lobster is cooked halfway through. Stir in the tomato purée and cook for another minute. Add the wine and cook until completely evaporated.

3 Add the cream, parsley and cheese and cook for about 5 minutes until the filling has thickened. The sauce should be pink and no longer watery. Leave to cool before filling the patties.

SEVEN-LAYER DIP WITH PLANTAIN CHIPS

This is what we Jamaicans would call very 'moreish' – meaning you just want more and more of it! For Caribbean flair, we add a double dose of plantains – in the corn salsa and for serving. We like Iselitas or Soldanas green plantain crisps, but go with what's available.

Serves 12

For the Corn and Plantain Salsa

1 x 400g or 2 x 198g cans sweetcorn kernels, drained
100g peeled and deseeded tomatoes, diced
2 tablespoons olive oil, plus more for tossing with the sweetcorn and tomatoes
2 tablespoons fresh basil, chopped
1 garlic clove, chopped
sea salt and freshly ground black pepper
80g peeled ripe plantain, chopped
2 tablespoons chopped spring onions
15g coriander leaves, roughly chopped
2 tablespoons lime juice

For the Tomato Coriander Salsa

170g plum tomatoes, without seeds, finely chopped
1 teaspoon finely chopped garlic
3 tablespoons olive oil, or more if needed
2 tablespoons chopped fresh coriander
sea salt and freshly ground black pepper

For the Chipotle Cream Cheese

450g cream cheese, at room temperature
240ml soured cream
1 x 210g or 198g can chipotle chillies/peppers in adobe sauce
1 bunch fresh coriander, chopped
sea salt and freshly ground black pepper

225g Cheddar cheese, grated
200g canned black beans, drained
55g pitted green or black olives, drained and sliced
1 avocado, stoned, peeled and sliced
225g feta cheese, crumbled
2 spring onions, chopped
1 handful fresh coriander leaves, chopped
shop-bought green plantain crisps, for serving

Method

1 First make the corn and plantain salsa. Preheat the oven to 190°C/gas mark 5. Toss the sweetcorn and tomatoes in some olive oil with the basil and garlic. Season with salt and pepper and roast in the oven for about 20 minutes until dry.

2 Meanwhile, combine all of the tomato coriander salsa ingredients in a small bowl and set aside for the flavours to develop.

3 Sauté the plantain in 1 tablespoon of the remaining olive oil in a small frying pan over a medium heat until golden brown. Transfer to a bowl and add the roasted sweetcorn and tomatoes, spring onions, coriander leaves, lime juice and the remaining 1 tablespoon oil. Season with salt and pepper.

4 Next make the chipotle cream cheese. Blend the cream cheese, soured cream and chipotle peppers together in a food processor. Add the chopped coriander and season with salt and pepper.

5 Spread the cream cheese onto a 30cm serving platter with sides to form the base. Top with the grated Cheddar, followed by the black beans, about 250g of the corn and plantain salsa, the tomato coriander salsa, olives, avocado, crumbled feta and spring onions, and finish with the coriander. Serve with the plantain crisps.

CARIBBEAN CROSTINI

Inspired by Italian antipasta platters, these crostini are brushed with a spicy herb oil, then heaped with your choice of topping: smoked marlin ceviche; curried ackee; spiced olives; or tomato, pepper and Scotch bonnet chokka. All of these versions have made regular appearances on our cocktail and buffet menus, and they're a great option if you're entertaining at home, too. Feel free to use the toppings on other recipes in this book, llike the flatbread on page 51 or the twice-fried pressed green plantains on page 138. The herb oil is great for dipping bread or flavouring pastas, so why not make a big batch?

Serves 12
For the Herb Oil
250ml extra virgin olive oil
2 garlic cloves, smashed
½ teaspoon sliced Scotch bonnet chilli
2 sprigs of fresh thyme
2 sprigs of fresh rosemary (or 1 tablespoon dried)
sea salt and freshly ground black pepper

toppings of your choice (recipes follow)
3 baguettes, sliced on a diagonal
sea salt

Method

1 To make the herb oil, combine the oil, garlic, Scotch bonnet, thyme and rosemary. Season with salt and pepper. Set aside for 30 minutes; the longer it sits, the better it will taste, so if you're making a big batch, refrigerate for up to 1 week.

2 Meanwhile, make your topping of choice, or all three.

3 When you're ready to assemble the crostini, preheat the oven to 180°C/gas mark 4. Brush the baguette slices with the herb oil and sprinkle with sea salt. Bake for 8–10 minutes until golden brown and crispy. Serve with the assorted toppings.

SPICED OLIVES

Makes about 750g
60ml olive oil
1 tablespoon ground cumin
2 teaspoons very finely chopped Scotch bonnet chilli
60ml fresh or carton orange juice
grated zest of 1 large orange
3 sprigs of fresh rosemary
2 bay leaves
2 tablespoons mixed peppercorns
700g mixed olives (Niçoise, Kalamata, green), drained and rinsed

Method

Put the oil, cumin, Scotch bonnet, orange juice and zest, rosemary, bay leaves and peppercorns in a container with a tightly fitting lid and shake well. Add the olives, cover and refrigerate for at least 24 hours before serving, or up to 3 weeks.

SMOKED MARLIN CEVICHE

Makes about 275g

225g smoked marlin, diced,
or any other type of smoked
fish, such as haddock or trout

1 spring onion, finely sliced

¼ red or yellow pepper,
finely chopped

¼ cucumber, deseeded and
finely chopped

1 tablespoon finely chopped
red onion

2 tablespoons chopped fresh
coriander leaves

3 tablespoons extra virgin
olive oil

2 tablespoons fresh lime juice

sea salt and freshly ground
black pepper

¼ teaspoon dried chilli flakes
or to taste

Method

Combine the smoked fish, spring onion,
pepper, cucumber, red onion and coriander in
a medium bowl. Stir in the olive oil and lime
juice, season with salt and pepper and add the
chilli flakes. Refrigerate for at least 4 hours to
allow the flavours to blend.

CURRIED ACKEE TOPPING

Makes about 275g

15g butter or 1 tablespoon
vegetable oil

4 teaspoons very finely
chopped garlic

2 tablespoons finely chopped
fresh thyme

1 teaspoon finely chopped
Scotch bonnet chilli

1 small onion, chopped

2 spring onions, chopped

½ red or green pepper,
chopped

450g ackee, picked and boiled
(see page 24), or 240g canned
ackee

sea salt and freshly ground
black pepper

1 teaspoon curry powder

2 tablespoons coconut milk
powder or 2 tablespoons
coconut milk

3 tablespoons freshly grated
Parmesan cheese

Method

Melt the butter or warm the oil in a medium
sauté pan and sauté the garlic, thyme, Scotch
bonnet, onion, spring onions and pepper for
2–3 minutes until soft. Add the ackee and
sauté for about 1 minute. Season with salt and
pepper and add the curry powder and coconut
milk powder or coconut milk. Cook for about
5 minutes, stirring occasionally, to allow the
flavours to blend. Remove the pan from the
heat and then fold in the Parmesan.

TOMATO, PEPPER AND SCOTCH BONNET CHOKKA

Makes about 250g

1 yellow pepper
6 plum tomatoes, quartered
½ red onion, sliced
4 whole garlic cloves, peeled
½ Scotch bonnet chilli, sliced
12 sprigs of fresh thyme
4 tablespoons extra virgin olive oil
2 tablespoons chopped fresh basil
2 tablespoons chopped fresh coriander
sea salt and freshly ground black pepper
1–2 teaspoons balsamic vinegar, or to taste
115g feta or soft goat's cheese, crumbled, for garnish

Method

1 Roast the yellow pepper over an open flame on the hob, rotating frequently, for about 10 minutes until the skin is charred but not burnt. Cover with clingfilm and leave to cool for about 15 minutes. When cool, peel the skin off the pepper; don't rinse it with water, as doing so will remove the flavour. Cut the roasted pepper into strips or large cubes, transfer to a medium bowl and set aside.

2 Preheat the oven to 200°C/gas mark 6.

3 Toss the tomatoes, red onion, garlic, Scotch bonnet and thyme with 2 tablespoons of the oil and 1 tablespoon each of the basil and coriander in a large bowl. Season with salt and pepper. Transfer to a baking tray and roast for about 20 minutes until the veggies are slightly caramelised. Leave to cool before roughly chopping the entire mixture.

4 Add the roasted tomato mixture to the roasted pepper; season with salt and pepper. Add the remaining 2 tablespoons oil, 1 tablespoon each basil and coriander and at least 1 teaspoon balsamic vinegar, and mix to combine. Sprinkle with the crumbled cheese and serve at room temperature.

ACKEE WONTONS WITH PAPAYA DIPPING SAUCE

This is one of our signature dishes. The flavour of the curried ackee filling combined with the Asian-inspired papaya dipping sauce is truly amazing. The wontons can be assembled and frozen ahead of time; that way, when you have some impromptu guests, you'll always have something on hand to pop in the fryer for a quick and easy snack.

Makes 48 wontons (serves 12)

2 tablespoons vegetable oil, plus more for deep-frying
½ small onion, finely chopped
3 garlic cloves, very finely chopped
1 spring onion, finely chopped
1 bunch fresh thyme, chopped
½ pepper, chopped
1 teaspoon finely chopped Scotch bonnet chilli
1 tablespoon curry powder
1 bunch fresh coriander, chopped
1 dozen fresh ackee, picked and boiled (see page 24), or
1 x 540g can ackee, drained
sea salt and freshly ground black pepper
48 wonton wrappers

For the Papaya Dipping Sauce

1 tablespoon toasted sesame oil
½ small onion, chopped
1 garlic clove, chopped
2.5cm fresh ginger, peeled and chopped
1 bunch fresh thyme
290g peeled and deseeded papaya, chopped
1 bunch fresh coriander, chopped
1 tablespoon distilled white vinegar
2 tablespoons fresh lime juice
1 tablespoon brown sugar
1 tablespoon honey
1 tablespoon Thai sweet chilli sauce
1 dash soy sauce

Method

1 Warm the 2 tablespoons vegetable oil in a large sauté pan over a medium heat. Sauté the onion, garlic, spring onion, thyme, pepper and Scotch bonnet for about 5 minutes until translucent. Add the curry powder and coriander and cook for about 1 minute until fragrant. Add the ackee and mix well. Season with salt and pepper.

2 To assemble the wontons, work with about four wonton wrappers at a time; keep the rest covered with a damp cloth so that they don't dry out. Spoon 1 rounded teaspoon of filling in the centre of each wonton wrapper. With dampened fingers (or a brush), wet the four edges of the wrapper and form a triangle by folding the dough in half over the filling, making sure the ends meet and the filling is centred; press down on the edges firmly to seal. Layer the finished wontons between greaseproof paper and freeze for up to 2 weeks.

3 To make the papaya dipping sauce, warm the sesame oil in a medium frying pan over a medium heat. Sauté the onion, garlic, ginger and thyme for 2–3 minutes until the onion is wilted and translucent. Add the papaya and coriander and cook for about 5 minutes until the papaya is tender. Add the vinegar, lime juice, brown sugar, honey, sweet chilli sauce and soy sauce and simmer for 10 minutes, stirring occasionally. Transfer to a blender and purée until smooth. Transfer to an airtight container and store in the fridge for up to 2 weeks.

4 When ready to deep-fry, heat 5–7.5cm of vegetable oil in a medium saucepan over a medium heat. Remove the wontons from the freezer, carefully drop them, in small batches, into the oil and fry until golden brown and crispy. Serve the wontons hot with the dipping sauce alongside.

SPICY BLACK BEAN AND CORN WONTONS WITH PAPAYA DIPPING SAUCE

These little dumplings meld Asian flavours like dark sesame oil and sweet chilli garlic sauce with traditional Tex-Mex ingredients like black beans, corn, fresh coriander, and chilli powder. Our papaya dipping sauce opposite is a perfect match for these wontons as well.

Makes 36 wontons (serves 12)

2 tablespoons toasted sesame oil
½ pepper, chopped
1 spring onion, diced
½ medium red onion, diced
2 garlic cloves, diced
1 tablespoon chilli powder
225g canned sweetcorn, drained
225g canned black beans, drained
1 bunch fresh coriander, chopped
sea salt and freshly ground black pepper
1 teaspoon Thai sweet chilli sauce
1 teaspoon rice vinegar
36 wonton wrappers
Papaya Dipping Sauce (recipe opposite)

Method

1 Heat the sesame oil in a medium saucepan. Add the pepper, spring onion, red onion, garlic and chilli powder and sauté for about 5 minutes, stirring frequently. Add the corn, black beans and coriander and stir until warmed. Season with salt and pepper.

2 Remove from the heat and mix in the sweet chilli sauce and rice vinegar. Assemble the wontons using 1 teaspoon filling, as described in step 2 of the recipe opposite. Fry the wontons as instructed in step 4. Serve with the papaya dipping sauce.

JERKED CHICKEN AND CASHEW SPRING ROLLS WITH PEANUT COCONUT DIPPING SAUCE

Building on the 'jam Asian' vibe, spring rolls are filled with classic Caribbean jerked chicken complemented by cashews and a tasty array of Asian seasonings. The sweet peanut coconut dipping sauce adds body, and balances the intensity of the spicy jerk seasoning.

Makes 24 small or 12 large spring rolls

350g boneless, skinless chicken breast, finely chopped
1½ tablespoons jerk seasoning, preferably Spur Tree or Walkerswood brand
2 teaspoons honey
1 tablespoon toasted sesame oil
1 teaspoon peeled and finely chopped fresh ginger
45g raw cashew nuts, toasted
1 tablespoon oyster sauce
2 spring onions, sliced
1 bunch fresh coriander, chopped
sea salt and freshly ground black pepper
24 small or 12 large spring roll wrappers
1 medium egg, beaten with 2 tablespoons water
475ml vegetable oil, for frying

For the Peanut Coconut Dipping Sauce
(MAKES ABOUT 180ML)
2 tablespoons hot water (or more as needed)
65g crunchy peanut butter
60ml canned or fresh coconut milk (see page 24)
1 tablespoon fresh lime juice
1 tablespoon brown sugar
1 teaspoon Thai sweet chilli sauce
2 teaspoons tamari
2 tablespoons raw cashew nuts
2 teaspoons chopped fresh coriander
1 tablespoon finely sliced spring onion

Method

1 Combine the chicken with the jerk seasoning and 1 teaspoon of the honey in a large bowl, tossing to coat.

2 Warm the sesame oil in a medium frying pan over a medium heat and sauté the chicken for 5 minutes, then add the ginger. When the chicken is fully cooked, add the toasted cashews, oyster sauce and the remaining 1 teaspoon honey. Cook for about 3 minutes until the chicken is browned, then stir in the spring onions and coriander. Season with salt and pepper and leave to cool.

3 To roll the spring rolls, brush both sides of one wrap with the egg wash. Place 2 tablespoons filling at one end of the wrapper. Fold in the sides, roll the spring roll and seal by brushing the loose end with a little egg wash. Repeat with the remaining wrappers and filling. (If not serving straight away, layer the spring rolls in an airtight container with greaseproof paper between the layers. Freeze for up to 2 weeks.)

4 To make the peanut coconut dipping sauce, whisk together the hot water and peanut butter in a bowl until smooth. Add the coconut milk, lime juice, brown sugar, sweet chilli sauce and tamari, and whisk until combined. (This sauce should have a dressing-like consistency, so add a little more coconut milk or water if necessary.) Toast the cashews in a small sauté pan until slightly charred, then roughly chop. Add the toasted cashews to the peanut sauce along with the coriander and spring onion and mix well.

5 When ready to serve, heat the vegetable oil in a large saucepan and fry the spring rolls until golden brown and crispy. Transfer to a kitchen paper-lined platter. Serve with the peanut coconut dipping sauce.

CALLALOO DIP WITH HOMEMADE ROOT CRISPS

What can we say about this dish except that it is blow-your-mind delicious? Our version of spinach and artichoke dip, the callaloo is intense and flavourful and provides creamy richness, but you can substitute kale or spring greens. For dipping, we give a recipe for homemade root vegetable crisps made from a mixture of sweet potato, green plantain and dasheen (also known as taro), but shop-bought sweet potato or pitta crisps or tortilla chips make great substitutions. This veggie purée also works well as a side dish.

Serves 12

4 tablespoons coconut oil
2 spring onions, chopped
8 garlic cloves, very finely chopped
1 medium onion, diced
1 Scotch bonnet chilli, deseeded and very finely chopped
1 bunch fresh thyme, chopped
1 bunch fresh callaloo, leaves stripped and thinly sliced (see page 23)
sea salt and freshly ground black pepper
475ml double cream
100g Parmesan cheese, freshly grated
45g panko (Japanese) breadcrumbs

For the Root Crisps

900g sweet potato, peeled
900g dasheen (taro), peeled
900g green plantain, peeled
950ml vegetable oil
sea salt and freshly ground black pepper

Method

1 Preheat the oven to 180°C/gas mark 4.

2 Heat 2 tablespoons of the coconut oil in a large frying pan over a medium heat. Sauté half the spring onions, garlic, onion, Scotch bonnet and thyme until softened. Add the callaloo and cook until wilted. Season with salt and pepper.

3 Heat the remaining 2 tablespoons coconut oil in a medium saucepan. Sauté the remaining spring onions, garlic, onion, Scotch bonnet and thyme. Stir in the cream and bring to a simmer, then reduce the heat and simmer for about 10 minutes until the cream is slightly thickened. Stir in half the Parmesan and turn off the heat. Season with salt and pepper, then add the cream sauce to the callaloo mixture.

4 Combine the remaining Parmesan with the panko in a small bowl. Pour the callaloo mixture into an ovenproof baking dish, sprinkle with the Parmesan-panko mixture and bake for about 30 minutes or until the top is golden brown.

5 Meanwhile, thinly slice the root vegetables lengthways on a mandolin and keep in a bowl of iced water until ready to fry.

6 Heat the vegetable oil in a large frying pan over a medium-high heat. Working in batches, take the sliced roots and pat dry. Slip into the frying pan, taking care not to overcrowd the pan, and deep-fry for 3–5 minutes until crispy and golden. Transfer to a tray lined with kitchen paper to drain. Season with salt and pepper and keep warm. Continue deep-frying until you've used up all the root vegetables.

7 Remove the dip from the oven and serve immediately with the root crisps.

CHO CHO COURGETTE-AND-MINT GAZPACHO

This soup is a refreshingly light change of pace from the typical hearty Jamaican soup. It's cool and clean-tasting – perfect on a hot summer day. Also known as chayote and similar to courgette, cho cho is used often in Caribbean cuisine. If you can't find chayote, butternut squash is a nice substitute here.

Serves 8

115g salted butter
2 medium onions, chopped
6 cho chos (chayote), peeled and roughly chopped (about 1.1kg)
3 courgettes, roughly chopped (about 1.1kg)
35g plain flour
20g chopped fresh mint leaves (or 3 teaspoons dried), plus fresh leaves for garnish
sea salt and freshly ground black pepper
2 litres warm water
15g chopped fresh coriander (plus more as needed)
3 tablespoons fresh lime juice (plus more as needed)
soured cream or chopped avocado, for garnish

Method

1 Melt the butter in a medium saucepan over a medium heat. Add the onions, cho chos and courgettes, and sauté for 2–3 minutes until the onions are translucent. Add the flour and sauté, stirring constantly, until cooked. Add the mint, season with salt and pepper and cook for 5 minutes. Gradually add the warm water, stirring occasionally. When the vegetable mixture comes to the boil, reduce the heat and simmer for 15–20 minutes or until the vegetables are thoroughly cooked and the soup has thickened.

2 Transfer to a blender in batches and purée. Return to the pan over a medium heat. Stir in the coriander and lime juice. Taste and adjust the seasoning, adding more salt, pepper, coriander and lime juice as needed.

3 Transfer the soup to a stainless-steel bowl set in an ice bath and whisk until cooled. Refrigerate for at least 3 hours until the gazpacho is properly chilled. Serve garnished with a fresh mint leaf and a swirl of soured cream or chopped avocado.

ROASTED PEPPER AND PUMPKIN SOUP

The smoky sweetness from roasting pumpkin and peppers gives this soup great depth of flavour and is delicious! The calabaza pumpkin is most similar to the Jamaican, but any starchy squash can be used.

Serves 8

4 large red peppers
900g peeled and deseeded pumpkin, roughly chopped
2 small onions, roughly chopped
2 spring onions, chopped
8 garlic cloves
1 bunch fresh thyme
½ Scotch bonnet chilli, deseeded and sliced
60ml olive oil
sea salt and freshly ground black pepper
1 x 400ml can coconut milk
about 475ml vegetable stock or water

Method

1 Preheat the oven to 200°C/gas mark 6. Meanwhile, roast the red peppers over an open flame on the hob until the skin is charred. Wrap in clingfilm for 15 minutes, then peel and remove the seeds. Set aside.

2 Toss the pumpkin with the onions, spring onions, garlic, thyme, Scotch bonnet and oil in a large bowl. Season with salt and pepper and transfer to a baking tray. Roast for 20 minutes or until the pumpkin is fully cooked.

3 Purée the peppers and roasted pumpkin mixture with the coconut milk in a blender until smooth. Place in a large saucepan over a medium heat. Add the stock or water and cook until heated through. Season with salt and pepper. If the soup is too thick, add a little more stock or water. Serve hot.

CREAMY TOMATO AND SCOTCH BONNET SOUP

This cream of tomato soup is simple and delicious. The coconut milk gives it a slightly sweet flavour that tempers the spice of the Scotch bonnet. If you don't want the soup to be spicy, simply leave out the Scotch bonnet.

Serves 6

1 whole head garlic
3 tablespoons olive oil
24 plum tomatoes
1 medium onion, chopped
1 bunch spring onions, chopped
2 bunches fresh thyme
½ Scotch bonnet chilli, deseeded and chopped
2 tablespoons tomato purée
240ml water
sea salt and freshly ground black pepper
60ml canned coconut milk
1 teaspoon brown sugar

Method

1 Preheat the oven to 180°C/gas mark 4. Slice off the root end of the garlic, place in a small baking dish, drizzle with 1 tablespoon of the oil and roast for 20 minutes or until the garlic is tender when pierced with a knife.

2 Meanwhile, with a paring knife, cut an X at the top of each tomato. Sink the tomatoes in a saucepan of boiling water for 3–5 minutes until the skins begin to lift. Remove from the water and leave to cool. Peel the tomatoes, squeeze out their seeds and chop, reserving any liquid. Strain the liquid and set it and the tomatoes aside.

3 Warm the remaining 2 tablespoons oil in a large sauté pan over a medium heat. Add the onion, spring onions, thyme and Scotch bonnet and sauté until softened. Add the tomatoes and cook for 5 minutes. Stir in the tomato purée, water and tomato liquid. Season with salt and pepper and cook for 20 minutes until the tomatoes break down.

4 Squeeze the garlic from its skin and mash it with a little salt. Add the garlic to the soup, then transfer the soup to a blender and purée until very smooth. Return the soup to the pan over a medium heat. Stir in the coconut milk and brown sugar and simmer for about 8 minutes. Season again with salt and pepper and serve.

GINGERED PUMPKIN BISQUE

The ginger gives this soup a nice little kick so that it's spicy without too much heat. Although the sweet potato is sometimes referred to as 'yam', it is not the same. True yellow yam is a firmer and more starchy root vegetable, so make sure you are buying the right tuber for this recipe. As with the previous recipe, the calabaza pumpkin is most similar in texture to the Jamaican pumpkin, but feel free to use whatever starchy squash is available.

Serves 12

675g pumpkin, peeled, deseeded and chopped
450g yellow yam, peeled and diced
1 spring onion, chopped
1 whole Scotch bonnet chilli
225g cho chos (chayotes), peeled and chopped
225g carrots, peeled and chopped
1 tablespoon fresh thyme leaves
5cm fresh ginger, peeled and smashed
100g coconut milk powder or 2 x 400ml cans coconut milk
sea salt and freshly ground black pepper

For the Gingered Cream
4cm fresh ginger, peeled and finely grated
60ml double cream

Method

1 Combine the pumpkin, yam, spring onion, Scotch bonnet, cho chos, carrots, thyme and smashed ginger in a large saucepan. Add enough water to cover and bring to the boil over a high heat. Reduce the heat and simmer for 45 minutes, taking care not to burst the Scotch bonnet, until the pumpkin is soft and completely cooked through. Remove and discard the chilli.

2 Transfer the soup in batches to a blender and purée. Strain the pumpkin purée through a fine-mesh sieve, then return to the pan over a medium heat. Whisk in the coconut milk powder or coconut milk until smooth. Season with salt and pepper. If the soup needs further thickening, allow it to simmer and reduce some more.

3 To make the gingered cream, mix the ginger and cream together in a small saucepan and warm over a medium heat.

4 Serve the soup hot, garnished with a drizzle of the gingered cream.

THE LADIES' LUNCH

SALADS AND SANDWICHES

Over the years, we have catered for many showers, tea parties and brunches, and there is always something really satisfying about eating, drinking and chatting with the ladies in our life. This chapter, filled with salad and sandwich recipes, is dedicated to the beautiful women who have supported, taught and befriended us, and who love to lunch as much as we do. In particular, we pay homage to the doyenne of nouvelle Jamaican cuisine, the late Norma Shirley.

Norma's approach to Jamaican food was groundbreaking and memorable. She was the first woman to bring Jamaican cuisine to the world stage – a real pioneer. Her dishes radiated with flavour and were as bold and full of personality and flair as she was.

When you dined at any of Norma's restaurants, you would be sure to find a beautifully set table and exquisitely styled plates. You would also see her bustling between the kitchen and the front of the house dressed in her signature Caribbean style, with a headband and silver bangles. As young women working in food, we were awed and inspired by her presence, and touched by her consistent support and interest in us and in our business. She was a mentor and a teacher, quick to advise us and equally quick to endorse us. Plus, she was authentic, fun, feisty and loved to laugh – our kind of lady.

ISLAND CAPRESE WITH SCOTCH BONNET OIL, CHADON BENI OIL AND HONEY BALSAMIC REDUCTION

We love, love, love *insalata caprese*, that classic Mediterreanean salad of sliced mozzarella and tomatoes drizzled with a little olive oil and a sprinkling of salt. To kick it up with a little island 'flava', we add avocado and Scotch bonnet oil – it's super-simple and super-good! You can store these special oils in the fridge for up to 3 weeks. The Scotch bonnet oil will get hotter as it keeps, so you can strain out the seeds to take out some of the bite!

Serves 4–6

For the Scotch Bonnet Oil
(Makes about 250ml)
250ml olive oil
4 Scotch bonnet chillies, deseeded and chopped
2 teaspoons sea salt

For the Chadon Beni (Culantro) Oil
(Makes about 250ml)
250ml olive oil
20g fresh chadon beni (culantro) or coriander leaves
2 tablespoons fresh lime juice
2 teaspoons sea salt

For the Honey Balsamic Reduction
(Makes about 250ml)
250ml balsamic vinegar
60ml honey
2 tablespoons sugar

3 beef tomatoes, sliced
2 small avocados, stoned, peeled and sliced
225g fresh mozzarella, preferably buffalo, sliced
2 tablespoons finely sliced fresh basil
sea salt and freshly ground black pepper

Method

1 To make the Scotch bonnet oil, purée the oil, Scotch bonnets and salt in a blender until smooth; set aside.

2 To make the chadon beni oil, purée the oil, chadon beni or coriander leaves, lime juice and salt in a blender until smooth; set aside.

3 To make the balsamic reduction, combine the balsamic vinegar, honey and sugar in a small saucepan and bring to a simmer over a medium heat. Simmer for about 15 minutes until reduced and syrupy.

4 On a serving platter, arrange the tomatoes, avocados and mozzarella in overlapping layers. Garnish with the basil and season with a generous amount of salt and pepper. Drizzle with 2 tablespoons of the chadon beni oil, 1–2 tablespoons of the Scotch bonnet oil and 1 tablespoon of the honey balsamic reduction. The Scotch bonnet oil is spicy, so use at your own discretion! Serve immediately.

MIXED SALAD LEAVES WITH PLANTAINS, GOAT'S CHEESE AND CHERRY TOMATOES

This is, hands down, one of the most popular salads on our catering menus. The combination of ripe plantain with goat's cheese and a light citrus vinaigrette is delightful. Give it a try for a light lunch.

Serves 4–6

2 tablespoons orange marmalade
60ml orange juice
1 teaspoon brown sugar
2 tablespoons vegetable oil
1–2 ripe plantains, sliced 5mm thick on the diagonal (you should have 18 slices)
175g chèvre or any soft goat's cheese
½ medium red onion, thickly sliced
2 caps portobello mushrooms, cut into strips
1 tablespoon olive oil
2 teaspoons chopped fresh thyme
sea salt and freshly ground black pepper
175g mixed salad leaves
24 cherry or baby plum tomatoes, sliced in half

For the Citrus Vinaigrette
(Makes about 300ml)
juice of 6 oranges (about 180ml)
1 teaspoon grated orange zest
6 tablespoons olive oil
1½ tablespoons distilled white vinegar
1 tablespoon lime juice
1 teaspoon Dijon mustard
½ teaspoon sea salt
1 teaspoon freshly ground black pepper
1 teaspoon sugar

Method

1 Preheat the oven to 190°C/gas mark 5.

2 Whisk together the marmalade, orange juice and brown sugar in a small saucepan over a medium heat and bring to the boil. Reduce the heat and simmer for about 15 minutes or until the sauce thickens a bit.

3 Heat the vegetable oil in a frying pan and pan-fry the plantain slices for 5 minutes until golden. Drain on kitchen paper. Mound each plantain slice with ½ teaspoonful of the goat's cheese, drizzle with the marmalade glaze and arrange on a baking tray. Set aside.

4 Toss the onion and mushrooms with the olive oil, thyme and salt and pepper. Arrange in a single layer on a second baking tray. Roast the plantains and onion-mushroom mixture for 20 minutes until the plantains are caramelised and the onion-mushroom mixture is cooked through. Set both baking trays aside to cool.

5 Meanwhile, make the citrus vinaigrette. Whisk together the orange juice and zest, oil, vinegar, lime juice, mustard, salt, pepper and sugar in a medium bowl until well combined and thickened.

6 Place the salad leaves in a large bowl, season with salt and pepper and toss with the citrus vinaigrette. Divide the dressed salad between four to six plates. Top with the tomato halves and the roasted onions and mushrooms. Garnish each plate with three plantain and goat's cheese croûtons and serve.

RED, GREEN AND GOLD SALAD WITH TOASTED ALMONDS

When we are in the mood for something healthy, we make this salad – with or without the feta, depending on whether we are on or off cheese that day of the week. It makes a lovely, fresh, light lunch – especially on a hot day. Pickled vegetables are a mainstay in many Jamaican kitchens and kept as an accompaniment for meals. So use as many beetroot as you'd like for this salad and keep the rest.

Serves 6

For the Pickled Beetroot
120ml fresh lime juice
60ml distilled white vinegar
2 tablespoons sugar
120ml olive oil
1 tablespoon chopped garlic
1 tablespoon Dijon mustard
sea salt and freshly ground black pepper
6 small cooked beetroot, peeled and sliced
1 medium red onion, thinly sliced
1 bunch fresh coriander, chopped

For the Mango Vinaigrette
(Makes about 450ml)
120ml mango purée, preferably fresh
80ml distilled white vinegar
2 garlic cloves, diced
1 teaspoon Dijon mustard
250ml extra virgin olive oil
sea salt and ground white pepper

225g mixed salad leaves
1 medium mango, stoned, peeled and sliced
1 x 400g can chickpeas, drained
¼ medium red onion, thinly sliced
½ cucumber, cut into matchsticks
½ red pepper, cut into matchsticks
1 medium ripe avocado, stoned, peeled and sliced
115g feta cheese, crumbled
sea salt and freshly ground black pepper
3 tablespoons flaked almonds, toasted

Method

1 To make the marinade for the beetroot, whisk together the lime juice, vinegar, sugar, oil, garlic and mustard in a small bowl until blended. Season with salt and pepper. In a medium bowl, combine the beetroot and red onion, pour the dressing over the beetroot mixture and season again with salt and pepper. Stir in the coriander and leave to stand for at least 30 minutes or refrigerate for up to 1 week.

2 To make the mango vinaigrette, whisk together the mango purée, vinegar, garlic and mustard in small bowl. Gradually add the oil, whisking steadily until the vinaigrette thickens. Season with salt and white pepper.

3 To assemble the salad, place the salad leaves in a large salad bowl. Add the mango, chickpeas, red onion, cucumber, pepper and avocado. Add half the feta and season with salt and pepper. Drizzle with a liberal amount of mango vinaigrette and toss. Top with the beetroot, toasted almonds and the rest of the feta and serve immediately.

FLATBREAD WITH ROCKET, PROSCIUTTO, MANGO AND MANCHEGO

The combination of sweet mango and salty prosciutto makes a lovely – and surprising – pairing. If you're pressed for time or just feeling lazy, you can buy ready-made flatbread and focus your energy on the toppings.

Serves 8

For the Flatbread Dough
570g plain flour, plus more for dusting
2 teaspoons sea salt
1 sachet (7g) easy-blend dried yeast
180ml warm water
4 tablespoons olive oil
650ml cold water

For the Herb Oil
(MAKES ABOUT 250ML)
250ml extra virgin olive oil
1 tablespoon chopped fresh rosemary
1 tablespoon fresh thyme
1 tablespoon chopped garlic
1 tablespoon chopped fresh basil
sea salt

For the Caramelised Red Onion
2 tablespoons olive oil
1 red onion, thinly sliced
sea salt

sea salt
225g thinly sliced prosciutto
225g Manchego cheese, shaved
170g mango flesh, thinly sliced
115g rocket
freshly ground black pepper
1 tablespoon Honey Basalmic Reduction
(page 46), or to taste
8 tablespoons fresh basil leaves, torn

Method

1 To make the flatbread dough, in the bowl of a stand mixer fitted with the dough hook, mix the flour and salt together for about 1 minute until thoroughly incorporated. Meanwhile, place the yeast in a small bowl and whisk in the warm water, then 3 tablespoons of the oil. Leave the yeast to rest for about 10 minutes until it begins to foam, then pour into a well in the centre of the flour. Mix the flour and yeast solution until well incorporated. Add the cold water to the flour and mix again until the dough pulls together in a single, unified mass.

2 Turn the dough out onto a lightly floured surface and begin to knead, working the dough with the heel of your hand. Push outwards and pull the inside edge over the top. Repeat the process over and over to create a smooth ball of dough, free of stickiness. This should take 6–8 minutes. Brush a clean, stainless-steel bowl with the remaining 1 tablespoon oil and put the ball of dough in the bowl. Cover with a clean cloth and leave to rise at room temperature for about 1 hour until it has doubled in size.

3 Meanwhile, make the herb oil. Whisk together the oil, rosemary, thyme, basil and garlic in a small bowl. Season with salt and leave to stand for at least 1 hour to allow the flavours to develop. (You can also use a blender.)

4 To make the caramelised red onion, heat the oil in a medium sauté pan over a low heat, then add the onion and season with a little salt. Cook slowly for 15–20 minutes until the onion is caramelised and slightly sweet.

5 Divide the dough into 8 balls. (The balls of dough can be individually placed in freezer bags and frozen for up to 2 months.) Heat a griddle pan over a high heat (alternatively, you can cook the flatbread on a gas or charcoal barbecue). With a rolling pin, roll each ball into an oval shape. Brush with the herb oil, sprinkle with salt and chargrill on both sides until marked. Cover each flatbread with prosciutto slices and top with the cheese shavings and mango slices.

6 Season the rocket with salt and pepper, then toss with the honey balsamic reduction and herb oil to taste in a small bowl. Mound the rocket on top of the prosciutto, mango and cheese. Add the caramelised onion and basil and serve immediately.

CAESAR SALAD WITH SOLOMON GUNDY CAESAR VINAIGRETTE AND HARDO CROUTONS

One of our head chefs, Sandy Williams, came up with this innovative and tasty twist on the traditional salad. Essentially, we lighten up the traditional Caesar by removing the egg and adding some favourite Caribbean ingredients. The tart vinaigrette is inspired by Solomon Gundy, a Jamaican spread made from pickled herring that we use instead of the traditional anchovies. For a touch of sweetness, we top the salad with some hardo bread croûtons and round it off with shaved Parmesan. You can also add grilled chicken, prawns or bacon bits.

Serves 6

For the Hardo Bread Croûtons
5 slices Jamaican hardo bread or other firm white bread, cut into 1cm cubes
60ml olive oil
4 sprigs of fresh thyme, chopped
1 garlic clove, very finely chopped
sea salt and freshly ground black pepper

For the Solomon Gundy Vinaigrette
(MAKES ABOUT 475ML)
250ml olive oil
2 tablespoons Solomon Gundy, preferably Walkerswood
juice of 6 small limes (about 60ml)
5 tablespoons distilled white vinegar
1 tablespoon extra-strong mustard, like Colman's or Dijon
1 tablespoon brown sugar, plus more as needed
1 tablespoon chopped garlic
1 teaspoon freshly ground black pepper

1 head Cos lettuce, torn into pieces
115g Parmesan cheese, grated
sea salt and freshly ground black pepper

Method

1 To make the croûtons, preheat the oven to 200°C/gas mark 6. Toss the bread with the oil, thyme and garlic in a large bowl, and season with salt and pepper. Spread out on a baking tray and bake for 20–25 minutes until the croûtons are brown and crispy. Leave to cool.

2 Meanwhile, to make the vinaigrette, whisk together the oil, Solomon Gundy, lime juice, vinegar, mustard, brown sugar, garlic and pepper in a medium bowl until well combined (or you can whizz in a blender). Taste and adjust the seasoning, adding more brown sugar if necessary.

3 Place the lettuce in a salad bowl. Add half the Parmesan and half the croûtons. Season with salt and pepper. Toss with some of the dressing to taste – be careful not to overdress, as the dressing is very strong. Top with the remaining croûtons and Parmesan and serve immediately.

PRESSED HAM AND THREE-CHEESE SANDWICHES

This jazzy, sweet and spicy version of a grilled ham and cheese sandwich (or a *croque monsieur* without the béchamel) is a definite winner! Pepper jelly is a well-loved condiment used on cheese, sandwiches and meats throughout the Caribbean. It is a spicy but sweet jelly made from hot peppers.

Makes 4 sandwiches

1 tablespoon olive oil
2 medium onions, sliced
sea salt
175g honey-glazed ham or Black Forest ham, preferably freshly baked, thickly sliced
2 teaspoons honey
8 slices Jamaican hardo bread or other firm white bread
4 teaspoons Dijon mustard
175g Gruyère cheese, grated or thinly sliced
55g mozzarella, preferably buffalo, grated or thinly sliced
4 teaspoons hot pepper jelly
45g butter
4 tablespoons freshly grated Parmesan cheese

Method

1 Turn on the grill.

2 Warm the oil in a medium sauté pan over a medium heat. Add the onions, sprinkle with salt and cook, stirring occasionally, until browned and wilted. Transfer to a plate and set aside.

3 In the same pan, place the ham slices to warm. As the ham cooks, drizzle with the honey so that it becomes sticky and caramelised.

4 Spread one slice of bread with 1 teaspoon mustard. Layer one-fourth of the Gruyère on the mustard, top with some onions, one-fourth of the ham and then one-fourth of the mozzarella cheese. Spread 1 teaspoon pepper jelly on a second slice of bread and place it, jelly side down, on the mozzarella. Spread the top of each sandwich with about 1 teaspoon of the butter. Repeat to create four sandwiches in all.

5 Melt about 1 teaspoon butter in a clean non-stick sauté pan over a medium heat. Place one sandwich, buttered side up, in the pan and press and hold with the back of the spatula as the sandwich cooks. When the bread is nice and caramelised, flip the sandwich over and repeat on the other side. Once the cheese begins to melt and the bread is nice and crispy, transfer to a baking tray that has been brushed with a little butter. Repeat with more butter and the remaining sandwiches.

6 Top each sandwich with 1 tablespoon Parmesan and grill until the cheese is melted and slightly brown on top. (Depending on the grill, this could take anywhere from 2–8 minutes, so watch carefully!) Cut each sandwich in half and serve immediately.

JERKED HONEY-BACON CHEESEBURGER WITH SWEET POTATO FRIES

Everyone loves a great burger and this one is delicious. The jerk seasoning provides a nice kick of spice, while the bacon and caramelised onions contribute sweetness. We replace mayonnaise with a spicy aïoli, which adds a smooth creaminess to complement the jerk. We like to use coco bread, as it is softer and moister than a standard hamburger bun.

Makes 6 x 115g burgers

675g beef mince
2 tablespoons jerk seasoning
1 bunch fresh thyme
1 tablespoon olive oil
½ onion, very finely chopped, plus 2 onions, sliced
1 garlic clove, chopped
¼ teaspoon ground allspice
sea salt and freshly ground black pepper
2 tablespoons vegetable oil, plus more for brushing
115g bacon rashers, cut in half to fit on burgers
1 teaspoon honey
140g thinly sliced cheese of choice, such as Cheddar or Swiss
5 Jamaican coco breads or hamburger buns
lettuce, sliced tomato and sliced red onion, for garnish
Sweet Potato Fries with Spiced Salt and Spicy Ketchup (recipe opposite), for serving

For the Coriander-Habanero Aïoli

(MAKES ABOUT 350G)
225g mayonnaise
120ml soured cream
½ Scotch bonnet chilli, deseeded and very finely chopped
1 teaspoon grated orange zest
1 teaspoon grated lime zest
2 tablespoons lime juice
1 garlic clove, very finely chopped
2 tablespoons chopped spring onion
3 tablespoons chopped fresh coriander
sea salt

Method

1 Mix the beef mince with the jerk seasoning, thyme, olive oil, finely chopped onion, garlic and allspice in a large bowl. Season with salt and pepper. Line a baking tray with greaseproof paper. Form the beef mixture into six evenly sized patties and place them on the prepared baking tray.

2 Make the coriander-habanero aïoli. Stir together all the ingredients except the salt in a small bowl. Leave to stand for at least 30 minutes to allow the flavours to meld, then season with salt.

3 Warm the vegetable oil in a sauté pan over a low heat. Add the sliced onions and cook for 15–20 minutes until caramelised. Transfer the onions to a plate and set aside. Add the bacon to the same pan and cook, turning from time to time. After 7–8 minutes, when the bacon is almost cooked, drizzle over the honey so that it gets nice and sticky.

4 Heat a gas or charcoal barbecue or a griddle pan to a medium heat and preheat the oven to 180°C/gas mark 4. Place a baking tray in the oven to warm. Brush the barbecue rack or griddle pan with some oil. Add the burgers and cook to the desired doneness (3–5 minutes per side for medium or medium-well), then remove from the heat before cooked through. Top each burger with the honeyed bacon, caramelised onions and a slice of cheese and transfer to the warmed baking tray. Place the burgers in the oven just until the cheese melts.

5 Meanwhile, toast or chargrill the hamburger buns. Spread both sides of each bun with 1 tablespoon of the coriander-habanero aïoli. Top one side of each bun with a burger and place on a serving plate. Top the other side of each bun with a piece of lettuce, tomato and red onion and add to the plate. Serve with the sweet potato fries and spicy ketchup.

SWEET POTATO FRIES WITH SPICY KETCHUP AND SPICED SALT

For the Spiced Salt
3 tablespoons fine sea salt
1 tablespoon chopped fresh thyme
½ teaspoon ground cumin
½ teaspoon ground allspice

For the Spicy Ketchup
240g tomato ketchup
1 tablespoon Pickapeppa sauce
2 teaspoons hot pepper sauce

475ml vegetable oil
2 large sweet potatoes, very thinly sliced into fine matchsticks (shoestrings), soaked in salted water, then drained and patted dry

Method

1 To make the spiced salt, toss together the salt, thyme, cumin and allspice in a small bowl. Transfer to a tightly sealed container. The salt will keep for up to 3 months.

2 To make the spicy ketchup, stir together the ketchup, Pickapeppa sauce and hot pepper sauce in a medium bowl. Transfer to a tightly sealed container. The ketchup will keep for up to 3 months in the fridge.

3 Heat the oil in a wide-based saucepan over a medium heat. To test the oil, drop in 1 sweet potato matchstick and see if it fries until brown. When the oil is heated enough, add the rest of the sweet potato fries in batches and fry for about 10 minutes until golden brown. Transfer to kitchen paper to drain, then fry a second time for about 5 minutes. Season with the spiced salt while still hot. Serve with the spicy ketchup.

SMOKED MARLIN AND CREAM CHEESE WITH ONION PICKLE À LA CAFÉ BELLA

People used to tell us that they dreamt about this smoked marlin sandwich, which is the original recipe for the first sandwich we ever served. Our café was located just down the road from the Bob Marley Museum, where the Marley family members spent their days. They regularly called us at around 11.30am, ordering anywhere from 7 to 20 marlin sandwiches for lunch, and sent someone to collect them within 15 minutes. To say that they loved this sandwich would be an understatement! If marlin is not readily available, use another smoked fish, such as smoked trout.

Makes 4 sandwiches

4 small onions, very thinly sliced
4 tablespoons capers, drained
240ml distilled white vinegar
50g sugar
450g cream cheese, softened at room temperature
240ml soured cream
1 tablespoon fresh dill or coriander leaves, chopped, plus more for garnish
sea salt and freshly ground black pepper
8 slices crusty wholegrain bread or baguette
225g smoked marlin or another smoked fish, such as smoked trout
4 lime wedges

Method

1 Mix together the onions, capers, vinegar and sugar in a small bowl and leave to stand for at least 1 hour. The pickled onions can be kept in the fridge for up to 1 week – you can simply keep adding fresh onions to the pickling marinade.

2 In a separate small bowl, put the cream cheese, soured cream, dill or coriander and pinches of salt and pepper, and mix well with a wooden spoon. (Alternatively, you can blend in a food processor.)

3 Toast the bread and spread 1 tablespoon of the cream cheese blend on each slice. Layer the marlin or other smoked fish thinly on top of the cream cheese on all eight slices. Top with freshly ground black pepper and a squeeze of fresh lime. Serve open-faced, garnished generously with the pickled onions.

SMOKED TURKEY AND BRIE

Our original recipe for this used honey mustard, which we later replaced with a sorrel chutney for a slightly more Caribbean taste. Here we combine the two. If you can't find sorrel chutney, mango will do.

Makes 4 sandwiches

2 tablespoons honey
2 tablespoons Dijon mustard
2 baguettes, cut into 15cm portions, each portion split open like a book
115g Brie cheese, cut into 4 thick slices
175g good-quality smoked turkey breast, thinly sliced
sea salt and freshly ground black pepper
½ small onion, thinly sliced
2 beef tomatoes, sliced
4 lettuce leaves
4 tablespoons red wine vinaigrette (page 181)
sorrel or mango chutney, to taste (optional)

Method

1 Preheat the oven to 190°C/gas mark 5. Mix together the honey and mustard in a small bowl and set aside.

2 Top one side of each baguette portion with one-quarter of the Brie and place on a baking tray. Lightly toast in the oven until the Brie is melted.

3 Divide the turkey slices on top of the melted Brie, sprinkle with salt and pepper and drizzle with the honey mustard. Top each sandwich with onion and tomato slices and a lettuce leaf, and drizzle with the vinaigrette. If using the chutney, spread it on the other side of each portion of bread. Close each sandwich and slice on the diagonal to serve.

SAUTÉED STEAK AND CHEESE SANDWICHES

Mummy used to make this signature sandwich for us; the combination of the Pickapeppa sauce with the mayo and onions is to die for!

Makes 4 sandwiches

1 bunch fresh thyme
2 garlic cloves, chopped
1 teaspoon peeled and grated fresh ginger
½ Scotch bonnet chilli, deseeded and finely chopped
1 bunch spring onions, sliced
2 tablespoons soy sauce
1 teaspoon brown sugar
225g fillet steak, cut into strips
3 tablespoons olive oil
2 medium onions, sliced
115g Emmenthal cheese, thinly sliced
8 slices Jamaican hardo bread or other firm white bread
4 tablespoons mayonnaise
4 teaspoons Dijon mustard
4 teaspoons Pickapeppa sauce
4 lettuce leaves (optional)
8 slices tomato (optional)

Method

1 Mix together the thyme, garlic, ginger, Scotch bonnet, spring onions, soy sauce and sugar in a bowl. Add the steak and marinate for 15 minutes.

2 Meanwhile, heat 1 tablespoon of the oil in a large frying pan over a medium heat. Add the onions, sprinkle with salt and sauté until browned and softened. Transfer to a plate and set aside.

3 Preheat the oven to 190°C/gas mark 5. Add another 1 tablespoon oil to the pan over a high heat. Stir-fry the beef in batches (adding the last tablespoon oil in between). After 2–3 minutes, when the beef is brown outside and tender inside, remove from the pan – don't overcook!

4 Divide the cheese between four bread slices. Toast all the bread (including those with no cheese) in the oven until the cheese is melted.

5 Spread 1 tablespoon of the mayonnaise and 1 teaspoon of the mustard on the non-cheesy slices of bread. Add the steak and onions. Drizzle the steak with 1 teaspoon Pickapeppa sauce, add the lettuce and tomatoes, if using, and cover with the cheesy slices of bread. Cut each sandwich in half and serve immediately.

CALLALOO STRUDEL WITH CREAM CHEESE À LA RED BONES

This dish is an homage to one of our longtime favourite dining spots in Kingston: the Red Bones Blues Café. This dish has been on their menu for as long as the restaurant has been open, and we order it every time we go there! This is our version of it. If you can't find callaloo, you can substitute spinach or kale.

Serves 4–6

1 tablespoon olive oil
1 garlic clove, chopped
1 small onion, chopped
½ Scotch bonnet chilli, deseeded and diced
1 bunch fresh thyme, chopped
1 spring onion, chopped
1 bunch callaloo, leaves stripped and finely sliced (see page 23)
250g ricotta cheese
sea salt and freshly ground black pepper
8 sheets thawed frozen filo pastry
115g butter, melted, plus more for greasing
225g cream cheese

For the Cream Sauce

240ml double cream
2 tablespoons fresh lime juice
2 tablespoons sliced spring onion
sea salt and freshly ground black pepper

Method

1 Preheat the oven to 190°C/gas mark 5.

2 Warm the oil in a large frying pan over a medium heat. Add the garlic, onion, Scotch bonnet, thyme and spring onion and cook, stirring occasionally, for 2–3 minutes until soft. Add the callaloo and cook, stirring occasionally, for about 3 minutes until it turns bright green. Transfer the callaloo mixture to a sieve and squeeze out all the excess water. Set aside to cool, then transfer to a large bowl and mix in the ricotta. Season with salt and pepper.

3 Place one sheet of filo pastry on a dry surface (cover the remaining sheets with a damp cloth so that they do not dry out). Brush the pastry with the melted butter, starting at the ends, which tend to dry out first. Place another layer of filo on top and brush again with butter. Repeat with all eight sheets.

4 Cut the cream cheese into four slices and arrange side by side on the filo, about 7.5cm from the edge. Top with the callaloo filling. Roll one edge of the filo over the callaloo mixture and keep rolling until the filo is all rolled up to form a log. Make sure you end with the cream cheese at the bottom of the log; if not, cut away the excess dough. Brush the seam with melted butter to seal.

5 Place the filo roll, seam side down, on a greased baking tray. Using a sharp knife, score the top of the filo to make it easier to slice the strudel neatly after baking. Brush the top of the strudel with more melted butter and bake for 25–30 minutes until lightly browned on top.

6 Meanwhile, to make the cream sauce, bring the cream to the boil in a small saucepan over a medium heat. Add the lime juice, reduce the heat and simmer for about 15 minutes until the cream has reduced and thickened. Mix in the spring onion and season with salt and pepper.

7 To serve, ladle the cream sauce onto four to six heated plates, slice the strudel and place a piece on each plate.

PRAWN SALAD WITH BLACK BEANS, CORN, PLANTAINS AND CORIANDER

Just one word for you: yummmmmm! Prawns are a very popular shellfish eaten throughout all the Caribbean islands; Jamaicans particularly love them. We always had to find ways to incorporate prawns into our buffet recipes. This prawn marinade also makes incredibly tasty grilled prawns on their own.

Serves 6–8

juice of ½ orange
juice of 1 lime
1¼ teaspoons cayenne pepper
1 teaspoon chilli powder
1½ teaspoons ground cumin
2 garlic cloves, chopped
1 teaspoon peeled and grated fresh ginger
1 tablespoon honey
2 tablespoons olive oil
sea salt and freshly ground black pepper
1 bunch fresh coriander, chopped, plus 15g chopped
450g fresh or thawed frozen raw king prawns (21–25), peeled and deveined, tails left on
2 tablespoons vegetable oil, plus more as needed
1 small ripe plantain, cut into cubes
½ red onion, chopped
1 spring onion, thinly sliced
½ red pepper, chopped
1 x 400g can black beans, drained
165g drained canned sweetcorn kernels
Lime Vinaigrette (page 75)

Method

1 Put the orange and lime juices, 1 teaspoon of the cayenne, the chilli powder, 1 teaspoon of the cumin, the garlic, ginger, honey, olive oil, salt and pepper and bunch of coriander in a food processor or blender and blend. Transfer to a baking dish or resealable plastic bag, add the prawns and leave to marinate in the fridge for at least 1 hour.

2 Warm the vegetable oil in a large frying pan over a medium heat. Add the plantain and sauté until caramelised and cooked through. Transfer to a large bowl and set aside. In the same pan, sauté the onion, spring onion and pepper for 2–3 minutes, then add to the bowl with the plantains.

3 Add a little more oil to the pan and stir-fry the prawns until opaque. (Alternatively, you can grill or barbecue the prawns.)

4 While still warm, add the prawns to the bowl with the vegetables. Add the black beans, sweetcorn, chopped coriander and remaining ½ teaspoon cumin and ¼ teaspoon cayenne. Add the vinaigrette, toss to combine and season with salt and pepper. Leave to rest for at least 30 minutes before serving to allow the flavours to develop.

CIAO BELLA

WICKED PASTA, ISLAND STYLE

Three visits to Italy during our teens and early twenties solidified our love affair with *La Bella Italia* – its culture, people, lifestyle and food. Much comes to mind when we think of Italy: the enthusiasm and zest for life, the crazy driving, the catcalls from the men in the streets and, of course, the mouthwatering food! We loved Italy so much that we decided to name our business Ciao Bella. We even made the Italian approach to life the basis for our first advertising campaign, using the tag line 'Hello, beautiful' to introduce our brand. Beauty is, after all, what Italy is all about: beautiful people, beautiful food, beautiful architecture, beautiful art – there is beauty every place you look!

On one of our early trips to Italy, we formed a relationship with a wonderful Italian family who had ties to Jamaica. They generously offered us hands-on instruction and insights on cooking and eating the Italian way. In their villa outside of Rome and at their grandmother's house in Forte dei Marmi, we cooked pasta, fresh pizza (in their outdoor brick oven), bruschetta and tiramisu. We dined al fresco in their garden, under the stars, and a great and long-lasting friendship developed. We thank the Alfano family for this formidable culinary experience, which has influenced all that we have cooked, both professionally and at home, ever since.

Our time cooking and eating in Italy inspired us to develop many inventive pasta dishes based on Jamaican ingredients. In fact, these wicked island-style pasta dishes have become our signature, and we've had loads of fun creating and serving them. We share our all-time favourites with you here.

PENNE WITH ACKEE AND COCONUT CREAM SAUCE

This pasta was a favourite dish throughout our years in catering. It was a hit at every event, and always created quite a stir when our guests realised that ackee could be used in such an original and unexpected way. The combination of ackee paired with thyme, Scotch bonnet and Parmesan cheese in a coconut cream sauce is delectable in a subtly exotic way.

Serves 6

2 tablespoons olive oil
1 medium onion, chopped
1 spring onion, chopped
3 garlic cloves, very finely chopped
½ teaspoon deseeded and very finely chopped Scotch bonnet chilli
2 tablespoons chopped fresh thyme leaves, plus 6 sprigs for garnish
2 tablespoons chopped pepper
2 small plum tomatoes, peeled, deseeded and diced
490g canned ackee, drained
sea salt and freshly ground black pepper
120ml canned coconut milk
350ml double cream
1 x 500g packet penne pasta
75g Parmesan cheese, freshly grated

Method

1 Heat the oil in saucepan over a medium heat. Add the onion and cook for about 5 minutes until softened. Add the spring onion, garlic, Scotch bonnet, thyme and pepper and cook, stirring occasionally, until the pepper is soft. Add the tomatoes, and when they begin to look cooked, fold in the ackee. Season with salt and pepper and cook for 2–3 minutes until the ackee is well seasoned and all the flavours are combined – don't stir too much! Add the coconut milk and bring to the boil. Add the cream and bring to the boil again, then reduce the heat to a simmer and cook until slightly thickened. Season again with salt and pepper, and then remove from the heat.

2 Cook the pasta in a large saucepan of salted boiling water until al dente, according to the packet instructions. Drain and return to the pan over a medium heat. Add the sauce and half the Parmesan, toss to combine and taste and adjust the seasoning as necessary.

3 Transfer the pasta to individual serving bowls. Garnish each serving with a sprig of thyme and sprinkle with the remaining Parmesan.

JERKED CHICKEN LASAGNA

This white lasagne, made with béchamel sauce, caramelised onions and bacon, and intensified by the spicy zip of jerked chicken breast, is sure to please almost any palate. And while there are many elements to this dish, once they are all prepared this is quick to put together.

Serves 10-12

6 boneless, skinless chicken breasts, 175–225g each, cut into strips
3 tablespoons jerk seasoning, preferably Walkerswood
3 tablespoons olive oil
8 garlic cloves, thinly sliced
6 medium onions, sliced
sea salt and freshly ground pepper
450g bacon rashers, chopped
1 x 500g packet lasagne sheets
15g butter
60ml white wine
240ml double cream
100g Parmesan cheese, freshly grated
115g mozzarella cheese, freshly grated

For the Béchamel Sauce

30g salted butter
1 teaspoon very finely chopped spring onion
1 teaspoon very finely chopped garlic
2 teaspoons fresh thyme leaves
2 teaspoons plain flour
240ml full-fat milk
240ml double cream
sea salt and freshly ground black pepper

Method

1 Put the chicken breasts with the jerk seasoning in a baking dish or resealable plastic bag and toss to ensure that the chicken is thoroughly coated. Leave to stand while you prepare the rest of the ingredients.

2 To make the béchamel sauce, melt the butter in a saucepan over a medium heat. Add the spring onion, garlic and thyme and cook for about 1 minute. Stir in the flour and cook for about 2 minutes until the flour is no longer raw tasting. Gradually add the milk and cream, a little at a time, whisking during each addition so that the sauce thickens but does not become lumpy. After about 5 minutes, when the sauce has thickened, season with salt and pepper and set aside.

3 Warm 1 tablespoon of the oil in a medium frying pan over a medium-high heat. Add the garlic and the chicken breasts and sauté for 5 minutes until the chicken is no longer pink. Transfer to a plate and set aside.

4 Add the remaining 2 tablespoons oil to a clean frying pan and warm over a medium heat. Add the onions and a sprinkle of salt. Reduce the heat and cook for 15–20 minutes until the onions are caramelised. Transfer to a plate and set aside. Add the bacon to the same pan and sauté for about 6 minutes until cooked. Transfer to a kitchen paper-lined plate and set aside.

5 Preheat the oven to 180°C/gas mark 4. Cook the lasagne sheets in a large saucepan of salted boiling water according to the packet instructions.

6 Meanwhile, melt the butter in a small saucepan over a medium heat. Add the wine and reduce by half. Pour in the cream and bring to the boil. Reduce the heat and simmer for about 10 minutes until thickened. Off the heat, stir in 25g of the Parmesan and set aside.

7 To assemble, spread a little of the béchamel sauce in the base of a lasagne dish. Follow with a third of the lasagne sheets, half the chicken strips, crumbled bacon and caramelised onions, and then top with a third of the remaining béchamel, Parmesan and mozzarella. Repeat the layers in the same order, ending with the final third of the lasagne sheets. Spread the remaining béchamel sauce over the entire dish and sprinkle with the remaining cheeses. Pour the cream sauce into the pockets of the lasagne.

8 Bake for about 25 minutes or until the cheese is browned and the lasagne is bubbly. Remove from the oven and leave to stand for about 10 minutes before serving.

CALLALOO AND RICOTTA RAVIOLI WITH TWO SAUCES

We served this dish for a wedding at the lighthouse in Negril. It was a beautiful but somewhat nerve-racking affair. The venue was spectacular, but it had no facilities, and we were serving a plated meal for two hundred people seated at long family-style tables – egad! As if that weren't challenging enough, the bride's Italian father was the producer of his own brand of olive oil and he wanted homemade ravioli with red and white sauce at the meal so much that he sent us recipes for the sauces. The pressure was on! We did not use his recipes, but instead came up with this version of the dish that incorporated some island flavour. The bride and groom were very happy, as was Papa.

COOKING HINT

Both of these sauces can stand on their own as a savoury complement to any type of pasta. They can be made ahead of time, as can the ravioli. Refrigerate each sauce in an airtight container for up to 5 days. Spread the uncooked ravioli on baking trays and place in the freezer. Once frozen, transfer the ravioli to an airtight container with greaseproof paper between each layer and freeze for up to 1 month.

Makes 24–30 raviolis (8–10 servings)

450g plain flour, plus more for dusting

sea salt

2 medium eggs

180ml warm water

3 tablespoons olive oil

½ onion, chopped

1 spring onion, chopped

3 garlic cloves, very finely chopped

¼ teaspoon very finely chopped Scotch bonnet chilli

1 bunch callaloo (or spinach, kale, rocket or spring greens), leaves stripped and finely sliced (see page 23)

sea salt and freshly ground black pepper

½ teaspoon freshly grated nutmeg

225g ricotta cheese

1 medium egg, beaten with 1 tablespoon water

freshly grated Parmesan cheese, torn fresh basil leaves and extra virgin olive oil, for garnish

For the Scotchie Arrabiata Sauce

2 tablespoons olive oil, plus more for drizzling

4 garlic cloves, chopped

1 Scotch bonnet chilli, deseeded and chopped

1 onion, chopped

1 bunch fresh thyme, chopped

12 plum tomatoes, peeled, deseeded and diced

1 x 400g can good-quality whole tomatoes, chopped

sea salt and freshly ground black pepper

For the Garlic and Thyme Cream Sauce

1 whole head garlic

1 tablespoon olive oil

30g butter

½ spring onion, finely chopped

½ small onion, finely chopped

1 bunch fresh thyme, chopped

120ml white wine

600ml double cream

Method

1 Sift the flour and ½ teaspoon salt into a large stainless-steel bowl. Make a crater in the centre and pour in the eggs and warm water. Using a fork, partially incorporate the flour into the liquid, then knead the dough for 4–5 minutes until well combined. Wrap in clingfilm and chill in the fridge.

2 Warm 2 tablespoons of the oil in a large sauté pan over a medium heat. Sweat the onion, spring onion, garlic and Scotch bonnet for 3–5 minutes. Add the callaloo and cook for about 5 minutes, then season with salt and pepper and the nutmeg. Transfer to a fine-mesh sieve and squeeze out any excess liquid. Transfer to a bowl and stir in the ricotta; taste and adjust for salt if necessary.

3 Remove the dough from the fridge and lightly dust a baking tray with flour. On a floured surface, roll out the dough 3mm thick. Working in batches, cut out approximately eight 7.5cm rounds. Place 1 teaspoon of the filling in the centre of four rounds. Brush another four rounds of dough with the egg wash and place on top of the filled rounds; press the edges of each ravioli together with the tines of a fork to seal. Set aside in a single layer on the prepared baking tray; if you stack the ravioli, they will stick together. Continue with the rounds, filling and egg wash until you've used up all the dough. Wrap the tray with clingfilm and freeze until ready to cook.

4 To make the Scotchie arrabiata sauce, warm the oil in a medium saucepan over a medium heat. Add the garlic, Scotch bonnet, onion and thyme and sauté for 5 minutes. Add the fresh plum tomatoes and their juices and cook for about 8 minutes. Stir in the canned tomatoes and their juice and bring to the boil. Reduce the heat to low and simmer for 20 minutes. Season with salt and pepper, remove from the heat and, using a blender, purée the sauce until smooth. Return the sauce to the pan over a low heat, add a drizzle of oil and adjust the seasoning. Keep warm.

5 To make the garlic and thyme cream sauce, preheat the oven to 200°C/gas mark 6. Chop the root end off the garlic, drizzle the whole head with the oil, wrap in foil and roast for 30 minutes until tender when pierced with a knife. Meanwhile, melt the butter in a medium saucepan over a medium heat, making sure it doesn't brown. Add the spring onion, onion and thyme and cook for 5–10 minutes until softened. Add the white wine and reduce by half. Add the cream and bring to the boil, then reduce the heat and simmer for 15–20 minutes until the sauce thickens. Remove the roasted garlic from the oven, squeeze the cloves out of their skins onto a chopping board and smash with the back of a spoon. Whisk into the sauce and simmer for 5 minutes. Keep warm.

6 When you are ready to cook the ravioli, bring a large saucepan of water to a rolling boil and add the remaining 1 tablespoon oil and 1 teaspoon salt. Add the ravioli and cook for 10–15 minutes until they float to the top. Using a slotted spoon, transfer to a colander to drain well.

7 Ladle the cream sauce into eight to ten warm pasta bowls to cover half of each bowl and the tomato sauce to cover the other half; the sauces should meet in the middle. Place three ravioli in each bowl on top of the sauces, garnish with Parmesan, fresh basil and a drizzle of extra virgin olive oil and serve.

PRIMAVERA JAMAICANA

This dish, which is our take on a traditional Italian primavera, was a hugely popular item back in the day at Café Bella – so much so that years later, when I was developing a menu for Usain Bolt's Tracks and Records, we rebirthed and revamped a version of it as Ital Penne with Pumpkin Rundown. At Café Bella, we used spinach fettuccine; feel free to use any pasta you like.

Serves 6

1 tablespoon olive oil
15g butter
1 bunch spring onions, sliced
2 garlic cloves, chopped
2.5cm fresh ginger, peeled and finely chopped
¼ Scotch bonnet chilli, deseeded and finely chopped
2 tablespoons chopped fresh thyme
½ red pepper, sliced
½ very ripe plantain, peeled and cut into cubes
125g peeled and deseeded calabaza pumpkin or other starchy squash, such as butternut, cut into matchsticks
1 cho cho (chayote), peeled and cut into matchsticks
55g green beans, trimmed
60ml Jamaican brandy or sherry
350ml double cream
1½ x 400ml cans coconut milk
25–50g Parmesan cheese, freshly grated, to taste
500g spinach fettuccine pasta
sea salt and freshly ground black pepper

Method

1 Warm the oil and butter in a large sauté pan over a medium heat. When the butter is melted, add the spring onions, garlic, ginger, Scotch bonnet, thyme and red pepper. Add the plantain and sauté for about 3 minutes. Add the pumpkin, cho cho and French beans. Add the brandy or sherry and cook for about 5 minutes until evaporated. Add the cream and reduce for 1–2 minutes, then add the coconut milk and cook until thickened. Stir in the Parmesan and set aside.

2 Cook the pasta in a large saucepan of salted boiling water until al dente according to the packet instructions. Drain and toss immediately with the vegetable mixture in the saucepan. Season again with salt and pepper and serve immediately.

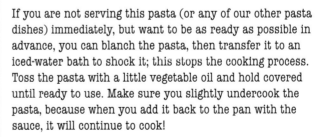

COOKING HINT

For extra kick-ass flavour, add 115g chopped bacon in step 1, along with the onions and peppers, and cook until crispy.

If you are not serving this pasta (or any of our other pasta dishes) immediately, but want to be as ready as possible in advance, you can blanch the pasta, then transfer it to an iced-water bath to shock it; this stops the cooking process. Toss the pasta with a little vegetable oil and hold covered until ready to use. Make sure you slightly undercook the pasta, because when you add it back to the pan with the sauce, it will continue to cook!

DOLCE JAMAICA

While we tend to prefer pasta with tomato sauce or simply tossed with some olive oil, it's just a fact that Jamaicans love creamy pasta sauces. This one is so yummy, with a hint of ginger and lots of fresh herbs, it's our go-to choice for last-minute entertaining or a simple dinner at home. It is easy, quick, appetising and always a hit.

Serves 4–6

juice of 2 limes
2 teaspoons peeled and grated fresh ginger
1 garlic clove, chopped
¼ Scotch bonnet chilli, deseeded and diced
2 tablespoons fresh thyme leaves
2 tablespoons chopped fresh mint
2 tablespoons chopped fresh coriander
3 tablespoons olive oil
sea salt and freshly ground black pepper
3 boneless, skinless chicken breasts, halved
1 x 500g packet penne pasta
35g Parmesan cheese, freshly grated, for garnish

For the Cream Sauce

30g butter
4 garlic cloves, very finely chopped
1 small onion, finely diced
1 spring onion, thinly sliced
¼ Scotch bonnet chilli, deseeded and finely diced
2 tablespoons fresh thyme, chopped, plus 4–6 fresh sprigs, for garnish
¼ portobello mushroom, chopped
sea salt and freshly ground black pepper
100g sun-dried tomatoes in oil, drained and sliced
120ml white wine
350ml double cream
35g Parmesan cheese, freshly grated

Method

1 Combine the lime juice, ginger, garlic, Scotch bonnet, thyme, mint, coriander, 1 tablespoon of the oil and salt and pepper in a baking dish or resealable plastic bag. Add the chicken and leave to marinate in the fridge for at least 1 hour.

2 To make the cream sauce, warm the butter in a medium saucepan over a medium heat. Add the garlic, onion, spring onion and Scotch bonnet and sauté for 3–5 minutes until the onion is translucent. Add the chopped thyme and mushroom with a dash of salt and cook for about 5 minutes until the mushroom is soft. Add the sun-dried tomatoes and white wine and simmer for about 2 minutes until the wine evaporates. Add the cream and bring to a simmer, then reduce the heat to low and simmer for 5–10 minutes until the sauce has thickened. Remove from the heat and stir in the Parmesan. Season with salt and pepper and keep warm.

3 Heat the remaining 2 tablespoons oil in a large sauté pan over a medium-high heat. Sear the chicken until brown on the outside and juicy on the inside – don't overcook! (Alternatively, cook the chicken in a griddle pan.) Transfer the chicken to a chopping board and cut into strips.

4 Cook the pasta in a large saucepan of salted boiling water according to the packet instructions until al dente. Drain, then immediately return to the pan, stir in the cream sauce and season with salt and pepper.

5 Divide the pasta and sauce between serving bowls. Top each serving with sliced chicken, a sprig of thyme and Parmesan and serve immediately.

ROASTED TOMATO, AUBERGINE AND CHILLI PASTA SALAD

Aubergines are called melangen in Trinidad and Tobago, and garden egg in Jamaica, where they grow easily but are not widely consumed, as many people don't understand how to prepare them. This quick and easy dish is delectable – and requires almost no washing up! It's a vegetarian option that everyone will love (for vegans, simply leave out the cheese), whether you're entertaining, eating a simple meal at home or need a dish to bring to an event.

Serves 6

2 small aubergines (about 450g total), sliced
8 plum tomatoes, quartered
2 onions, thickly sliced
8 garlic cloves, sliced
180ml olive oil (plus more if needed)
1 bunch fresh thyme, chopped
1 bunch fresh coriander, chopped (plus more if needed)
½ Scotch bonnet chilli, deseeded and sliced into thin slivers
sea salt and freshly ground black pepper
1 x 500g packet pasta of your choice
115g feta cheese, crumbled (optional)

Method

1 Preheat the oven to 190°C/gas mark 5.

2 Toss the aubergines, tomatoes, onions and garlic with the oil, thyme, coriander and Scotch bonnet in a large bowl. Season with salt and pepper, then transfer to a baking tray and spread out in a single layer. Roast the vegetables for about 30 minutes until the aubergine is moist and cooked through and the onions are caramelised.

3 Meanwhile, cook the pasta in a large saucepan of salted boiling water according to the packet instructions. Drain and leave to cool.

4 Roughly chop the roasted vegetables, then toss with the pasta in a large bowl. Add more coriander and oil, if necessary, then add the crumbled feta, if using, and toss to combine. Season with salt and pepper and serve at room temperature.

GINGER THYME RISOTTO

We blended Jamaican ginger with fresh thyme in this creamy risotto. It's scrumptious served as a side dish or on its own. Years ago, we paired it with fresh local marlin in a sherry glaze with grilled asparagus and crispy fried leeks alongside. But here we're giving it to you solo . . . so you can eat it alongside whatever you want.

Serves 10

85g butter
35g onion, chopped
3 tablespoons peeled and finely chopped fresh ginger
2 tablespoons finely chopped garlic
400g Arborio rice
120ml dry white wine
240ml sherry
1 litre hot chicken stock
3 tablespoons chopped fresh thyme (plus more as needed)
300ml double cream
50g Parmesan cheese, freshly grated
sea salt and freshly ground black pepper

Method

1 Melt the butter in a heavy-based saucepan over a medium heat. Add the onion, ginger and garlic and sweat for 1–2 minutes. Add the rice and cook, stirring frequently, until the tips of the rice appear white and all the grains are coated with oil. Add the white wine and 80ml of the sherry and cook, stirring frequently, until the liquid is almost evaporated.

2 Add about one-third of the stock to the pan, stirring until the liquid has been absorbed into the rice. Add the remaining stock in two more additions, stirring constantly, until the liquid is absorbed and the rice begins to develop a creamy texture.

3 Add the remaining sherry in the same manner, stirring constantly, and continue to cook until the rice is al dente and most of the liquid is absorbed; this should take 45–50 minutes in all.

4 Add the thyme, cream and Parmesan and stir until the risotto thickens again. Season to taste with salt and pepper, adjust the thyme, if necessary, and serve.

PASTA SALAD CUBANA À LA SUGARDADDIES

When we developed this menu item for a local Jamaican franchise, Sugardaddies, back in the year 2000, it was a novel dish indeed: penne with ripe plantain, lime vinaigrette, feta, black beans and corn. Ripe plantain is often featured in our dishes, in everything from salads to sandwiches to pastas and roasts. Sugardaddies is no longer around, but boy, we still get requests for this pasta recipe, so here it is! This is a vegetarian main course, but you can add grilled chicken breast to create a hearty pasta salad.

Serves 8–10

1 x 500g packet penne pasta
2 tablespoons vegetable oil
1 small ripe plantain, cut into cubes
250g drained canned black beans
85g drained canned sweetcorn kernels
½ red pepper, chopped
½ red onion, chopped
1 spring onion, thinly sliced
20g fresh coriander leaves, chopped
150g feta cheese, crumbled
sea salt and freshly ground black pepper

For the Lime Vinaigrette

2 tablespoons fresh lime juice
2 tablespoons olive oil
1 teaspoon ground cumin
2 tablespoons chopped fresh coriander leaves
1 teaspoon finely chopped garlic
sea salt and freshly ground pepper

Method

1 Cook the pasta in a large saucepan of salted boiling water according to the packet instructions. Drain and leave to cool.

2 Meanwhile, make the vinaigrette. Whisk together the lime juice, olive oil, cumin, coriander and garlic in a small bowl until well combined. Season with salt and pepper.

3 Warm the vegetable oil in a small sauté pan over a medium heat. Add the plantain and sauté for 5–10 minutes until golden. Leave to cool.

4 Combine the pasta, black beans, sweetcorn, plaintain, red pepper, red onion, spring onion, coriander and feta in a large salad bowl. Add the vinaigrette and toss to combine. Season with salt and pepper. Leave to stand for at least 15 minutes to allow the flavours to meld.

5 Toss the salad once again and serve at room temperature.

THE WICKEDEST RIGATONI ALLA VODKA

This has always been one of our absolutely favourite pastas; anywhere we go, if it's on the menu we must order it to share! We both love pink sauce for its depth of flavour. We use jerk sausage from a local smokehouse, but you can substitute any type of spicy sausage, such as chorizo. We add a dash of coconut milk for a hint of sweetness. If you want to add additional island flavour, substitute the Scotchie Arrabiata on page 67 for the basic tomato sauce (you'll need about 500g) but only if using the bacon.

Serves 4–6

For the Basic Tomato Sauce
2 tablespoons extra virgin olive oil
1 medium onion, finely chopped
1 garlic clove, crushed
2 x 400g cans whole tomatoes, chopped
120ml white wine
1 bunch fresh basil, chopped
1 teaspoon chopped fresh thyme
sea salt and freshly ground black pepper

For the Vodka Sauce
3 tablespoons olive oil
½ onion, chopped
115g bacon or spicy sausage, diced
3 garlic cloves, very finely chopped
2 tablespoons chopped fresh thyme
60ml vodka
60ml canned coconut milk (optional)
120–180ml double cream, depending on whether you use coconut milk
sea salt and freshly ground black pepper

1 x 500g packet rigatoni pasta
70g Parmesan cheese, freshly grated
3 tablespoons chopped fresh parsley

Method

1 To make the basic tomato sauce, warm the oil in a large saucepan over a medium heat. Add the onion and garlic and sweat for about 5 minutes. Add the tomatoes and their juice and bring to a simmer over a medium heat. Add the white wine, basil and thyme and return to a simmer. Reduce the heat to low and simmer gently, stirring occasionally, for about 30 minutes until the sauce is thickened. If the sauce becomes too dry and starts to stick to the sides of the pan, add a few tablespoons of water. Season with salt and pepper and remove from the heat. Purée with a hand blender or in a food processor and set aside.

2 To make the vodka sauce, warm the oil in a large frying pan over a medium heat. Add the onion and cook for 5 minutes. Add the bacon or sausage and cook for another 5 minutes, then add the garlic and thyme. Cook for about 6 minutes until the bacon or sausage is cooked through.

3 Add the vodka and reduce until there is about 1 tablespoon left. Add the tomato sauce and bring to a simmer. Add the coconut milk, if using, and cream and cook until thickened. Season with salt and pepper.

4 Meanwhile, cook the pasta in a large saucepan of salted boiling water according to the packet instructions. Drain and return to the pan. Add the vodka sauce and half the Parmesan and toss well.

5 Taste and adjust the salt and pepper as necessary. Mix in the parsley and serve topped with the remaining Parmesan.

SUNDAY SUPPERS

ROASTS, STEWS AND FIXINGS

Sundays in the Caribbean are about family. All across the islands, families either dress up in their Sunday best and head to church for a few hours of fervent worship, or head off to the beach for a leisurely day of chilling in the sun. Either way, these activities build up quite an appetite, so they are typically followed by a hearty lunch.

We have many a fond childhood memory of Sunday meals, which always consisted of a tasty roast (pork with crackling, beef, chicken or leg of lamb) served with roasted potatoes, rice and peas, fried ripe plantain, avocado, salad, macaroni pie and gravy. This was usually followed by a trip to the local ice cream parlour for a Sunday 'cream'. The lines were long, the wait eternal, but my-oh-my was it ever worth it!

In this chapter, we journey down memory lane and bring you some updated versions of our favourite Sunday lunches.

ROAST CHICKEN WITH CORNBREAD STUFFING

Every Caribbean island has its own version of roast chicken, and this is ours. We like to serve it with cornbread stuffing, as a change of pace from the white bread stuffing that is traditional. Serve with Rice and Peas (page 142), Rum Brown Sugar Plantains (page 128) and Twice-Roasted Local Mixed Vegetables (page 132).

Serves 6

5 garlic cloves, very finely chopped
2.5cm fresh ginger, peeled and grated
1 bunch fresh thyme, chopped
2 tablespoons soy sauce
1 tablespoon ground allspice
1 bunch spring onions, sliced
½ teaspoon ground cinnamon
1 teaspoon very finely chopped Scotch bonnet chilli
2 tablespoons olive oil
1 tablespoon brown sugar
sea salt and freshly ground black pepper
1 whole roasting chicken, 2.25kg

For the Cornbread Stuffing

1 box cornbread or corn muffin mix
15g butter
2 tablespoons olive oil
450g bacon rashers, chopped
70g chopped onion plus
1 small onion, sliced
50g celery, chopped
35g peeled carrot, chopped
2 garlic cloves, chopped, plus 2 whole cloves, peeled
1 bunch fresh thyme, chopped, plus 1 sprig
85g raisins
sea salt and freshly ground black pepper
2 plum tomatoes, chopped
1 whole Scotch bonnet chilli
sprig of fresh rosemary
3–4 tablespoons white wine, to taste
1 teaspoon brown sugar

Method

1 Put the garlic, ginger, thyme, soy sauce, allspice, spring onions, cinnamon, Scotch bonnet, oil, brown sugar and salt and pepper in a small bow and mix to form a paste. Rub the paste all over the chicken and inside the cavity. Leave the chicken to stand in the fridge for at least 1 hour (preferably overnight).

2 To make the stuffing, bake the cornbread or corn muffin mix in a baking tray according to the packet instructions. Leave to cool, then cut into 2.5cm cubes.

3 Preheat the oven to 200°C/gas mark 6.

4 Melt the butter with the oil in a large saucepan over a medium heat, then pour half the melted butter and oil mixture into a small bowl and reserve. In the butter and oil remaining in the pan, sauté the bacon for about 5 minutes until it begins to brown. Add the chopped onion, celery and carrot and cook for another 5 minutes, stirring occasionally. Add the chopped garlic, chopped thyme and raisins and cook for about 3 minutes. Add the cornbread cubes, stir to coat and season with salt and pepper. Remove from the heat.

5 Place half the stuffing in a serving dish; don't allow this stuffing to touch the raw chicken, as it will just be warmed for serving. Stuff the remaining half of the stuffing into the cavity of the chicken and place the chicken in a roasting tin, on a rack if desired. Pour the reserved butter and olive oil mixture over the chicken and roast for 15 minutes, then reduce the heat to 180°C/gas mark 4 and roast for another 30–35 minutes until the juices run clear when a knife tip is inserted into a leg joint (74°C on an instant-read thermometer). Transfer the chicken to a chopping board.

6 Transfer the pan juices to a saucepan. Add the tomatoes, sliced onion, garlic cloves, Scotch bonnet and thyme and rosemary sprigs and simmer over a medium-low heat for about 10 minutes until the vegetables are softened. Stir in the white wine and brown sugar and add water if necessary. Transfer the gravy to a serving bowl.

7 Remove the stuffing from the chicken and mound it in the centre of a platter. Carve the chicken and place alongside the stuffing. Serve with the extra stuffing and gravy on the side.

ROAST RIB OF BEEF WITH MUSHROOM GRAVY

Many summer holidays were spent in London with our aunt Winsome, who judged every event to be a success or failure by the quality and quantity of the food. She was known for her enormous appetite even though she was not overweight. Her daughter Caroline was our constant companion from as young as three years old to our early twenties, as our families went on holiday together. We shared many a meal of roast beef and Yorkshire pudding, which was, and still continues to be, a family favourite.

Serves 8-10

2 tablespoons soy sauce or Worcestershire sauce
4 tablespoons olive oil
1 bunch fresh rosemary, chopped
2 bunches fresh thyme, chopped
6 garlic cloves, very finely chopped
1 onion, finely chopped, plus 2 onions, quartered
½ Scotch bonnet chilli, deseeded and very finely chopped
sea salt and freshly ground black pepper
boneless rolled rib of beef joint, 3–3.6kg
6 small roasting potatoes, halved or quartered depending on size
8 large carrots, peeled and chopped
4 cho cho (chayote), peeled and chopped (see page 23)

For the Mushroom Gravy

60ml red wine
knob of butter
175g button mushrooms
1 handful shiitake mushroom caps
1 small onion, chopped
3 plum tomatoes, chopped
3 whole garlic cloves, peeled
240ml beef stock
½ teaspoon sugar
1 bay leaf
1 teaspoon cornflour mixed to a paste with 1 tablespoon cold water (optional)

Method

1 Mix together the soy or Worcestershire sauce, 2 tablespoons of the oil, the rosemary, 1 bunch of the thyme, the garlic, chopped onion, Scotch bonnet and salt and pepper in a small bowl to form a slightly wet paste. With a sharp knife, score holes in the beef and generously stuff the paste deep into the holes. Rub the remaining paste all over the exterior of the beef, followed by a generous rubbing with sea salt. Place the beef in a baking dish, cover with clingfilm and refrigerate for at least 12 hours. Remove from the fridge and leave for about 1 hour to come to room temperature before roasting.

2 Preheat the oven to 190°C/gas mark 5.

3 Transfer the beef to a rack in a roasting tin and then roast for about 30 minutes.

4 Meanwhile, toss the potatoes, carrots, quartered onions and cho cho with the remaining 2 tablespoons oil and the remaining bunch of thyme in a large bowl, and season with salt. After the beef has cooked for about 30 minutes, add the vegetables to the base of the roasting tin so that the dripping from the beef will baste the vegetables during cooking. Cook for another 40–45 minutes until the potatoes are fork-tender. Transfer the potatoes and other vegetables to a plate and test the meat with an instant-read thermometer inserted into the thickest part. If it reads 60–63°C, you'll have a medium doneness. Transfer the meat to a chopping board.

5 To make the mushroom gravy, place the roasting tin with the pan juices on the hob. Skim off any excess fat, then add the red wine and deglaze the pan. Add the knob of butter along with the mushrooms, onion, tomatoes and garlic cloves and cook for about 5 minutes. Add the beef stock, sugar and bay leaf and simmer for another 10 minutes until it thickens slightly. If you want to thicken the gravy further, whisk in the cornflour paste.

6 Carve the beef and serve with the roasted vegetables and mushroom gravy on the side.

MUMMY'S ROAST PORK WITH CRACKLIN' AND RUM GRAVY

Our mother is a master at making roast pork with cracklin'. The cracklin' is always absolutely perfect, and though we know all too well that it might not be good for the heart, there is literally a fight for the cracklin' when it comes out of the oven. Mummy now hides it until it's time to eat. Between Liam, Jude (a self-declared carnivore) and our father, the likelihood of the ladies even getting one bite of the cracklin' is slim to none – which is why it's always good to know where the hiding spot is so we can 'teif' a little! Here is Mummy's technique for outrageously good cracklin', every single time.

Serves 8-10

2.5cm fresh ginger, peeled and roughly chopped
4 garlic cloves, roughly chopped, plus 8 whole cloves, peeled
2 bunches fresh thyme, roughly chopped
2 spring onions, roughly chopped
¼ small onion, roughly chopped, plus 1 large onion, quartered
½ Scotch bonnet chilli, deseeded and chopped, plus 1 whole
sea salt
1 tablespoon olive oil
2 tablespoons soy sauce
leg of pork joint with a good skin and fat, about 3.6kg
4–6 limes
6–8 potatoes, quartered, with skin on
1 tablespoon chopped fresh rosemary
freshly ground black pepper
2 bay leaves
3 tablespoons rum
3 plum tomatoes, chopped

Method

1 Put the ginger, chopped garlic, half the thyme, the spring onions, chopped onion, chopped Scotch bonnet, 2 teaspoons salt, the oil and 1 tablespoon of the soy sauce in a food processor or blender and blend to form a paste. Using a sharp knife, score holes all over the pork leg and stuff the paste into the holes. Rub the remaining paste to coat the outside of the meat. Place the pork leg, skin side up, in a roasting pan and pat the fat dry – be sure not to place it skin side down, where it may soak in liquid, or you won't achieve successful cracklin'. Refrigerate, uncovered, for at least 4 hours, to allow the skin to dry out.

2 Preheat the oven to 260°C, or 240°C/gas mark 9 if that's the highest setting you have. Remove the chilled pork from the fridge, pat the skin dry again and score lines in the skin in a criss-cross pattern. Squeeze the limes onto the skin, then rub generously with a little less than 1 tablespoon salt. Repeat this process five times: squeezing lime juice onto the skin, then rubbing it with salt. Place the pork on a rack in a roasting tin, then place the cold meat in a piping hot oven (the heat will draw the fat out of the skin and make the cracklin' good and crispy). Roast the pork for about 40 minutes. Do not turn the pork or baste it; it must stay skin side up.

3 Meanwhile, toss the potatoes with the rosemary, quartered onion and salt and pepper to taste in a large bowl and set aside.

4 The cracklin' will finish cooking before the pork. After about 30 minutes, you will see the skin of the pork beginning to bubble. After 40–45 minutes, when the skin is bubbly, brown and crispy around the edges, the cracklin' is done. Remove the meat from the oven and cut away the skin from the leg, leaving some fat on top of the leg. (It should come off easily, as the skin will have separated from the fat by now.)

5 Reduce the oven temperature to 200°C/gas mark 6. Pour out all the pan juices from the base of the roasting tin into a measuring jug and skim off the excess fat. Take 2 tablespoons of this pork fat and toss with the

seasoned potatoes and onion. Place the pork in the centre of the pan without
the rack with the potatoes and onions surrounding it. Pour the rest of the pan
juices over the pork and potatoes and return the pan to the oven. Cook the pork,
turning and basting as necessary, for about a further 1½ hours or until the meat
is cooked through and an instant-read thermometer inserted into the thickest
part of the leg registers at least 71°C. Transfer the meat to a chopping board and
the vegetables to a plate and set aside.

6 If there is a lot of fat in the pan juices, pour the cooking liquid into a glass jar
or bowl and place in the fridge. Once it has cooled a little, skim the fat off the
top of the juices and place the juices in a saucepan. Add the garlic cloves, the
remaining thyme, the bay leaves, the whole Scotch bonnet, the remaining
1 tablespoon soy sauce, the rum and tomatoes and simmer for about 15 minutes
until the tomatoes are cooked.

7 Carve the pork and place it on a platter, mounding the potatoes and onions
around the meat. Chop the cracklin' and arrange it around the edges of the
platter as a garnish. Serve with the gravy on the side.

BAKED HAM WITH ORTANIQUE GINGER GLAZE

We always make this wonderful ham leading into the holiday season, and while our family doesn't serve ham at Christmas dinner, we keep this in the fridge for a quick meal and an even quicker sandwich. The ham bone makes an awesomely delicious gungo (pigeon) pea soup that's perfect for Boxing Day lunch. Extremely sweet, an ortanique is a cross between a Valencia orange and a tangerine; if you aren't lucky enough to find one, substitute another sweet orange instead.

Serves 12

1 bone-in ham joint, 5.5–6.8kg, presoaked in cold water if necessary (ask your supplier if the ham needs soaking and for how long, depending on the curing)
2 handfuls allspice berries
2 handfuls whole cloves
1 handful black peppercorns
2 bay leaves
3 tablespoons grated ortanique or orange zest, plus 1 handful thin strips
210g brown sugar, plus 3 tablespoons and more for sprinkling
5cm fresh ginger, half roughly chopped, half peeled and grated
720ml fresh ortanique or orange juice
125g Dijon mustard, plus more for serving
1 ortanique or orange, sliced
fruit chutney, for serving

Method

1 Put the ham in a very large saucepan and cover with fresh cold water. Add 1 handful of the allspice, 1 handful of the cloves, the peppercorns, bay leaves, the strips of ortanique or orange zest, the 3 tablespoons brown sugar and the roughly chopped ginger. Slowly bring to the boil, skimming off any scum from the surface. Reduce the heat and simmer gently for 20 minutes per 450g.

2 Turn off the heat and leave the ham to cool in the cooking liquid for about 30 minutes or just until cool enough to handle. Meanwhile, preheat the oven to 180°C/gas mark 4.

3 Lift the ham out of the cooking liquid onto a chopping board. Peel the skin off the ham and score the fat in a diamond shape.

4 Simmer the grated ortanique or orange zest and juice, the 210g brown sugar, the grated ginger and remaining 1 handful allspice in a small saucepan over a medium heat for about 15 minutes until the sugar is melted and the glaze is slightly thickened.

5 Set the ham in a baking dish, spread the top with the mustard and sprinkle with some brown sugar. Insert the remaining 1 handful cloves in the top of the ham. Pour half the glaze over the ham.

6 Bake the ham for 1½ hours, basting frequently with the glaze. In the last 30 minutes, add the ortanique or orange slices to the top of the ham in a decorative pattern, securing them with wooden cocktail sticks. Bake and baste until the top of the ham is caramelised and sticky.

7 Transfer the juices from the bottom of the pan to a sauce bowl. Carve the ham and garnish with ortanique or orange slices. Place the ham on a platter and serve with Dijon mustard, fruit chutney and the pan juices on the side.

SUZIE'S SUNDAY ROAST PORK CHOPS

So here's the thing: I love turning up unannounced at my sister's house on a Sunday because there is always the most delightful spread and I get to (selfishly) indulge without doing any of the work. Suzie's pork chops are infamous – they're simple and absolutely delicious with the combination of Asian flavours and surprise burst of mint. All I have to do is arrive and settle in like one of the kids, extending my plate for seconds when the time comes. – MICHELLE

Serves 4–6

1 teaspoon grated orange zest
60ml orange juice
2 tablespoons peeled and grated fresh ginger
2 tablespoons soy sauce
1 bunch fresh coriander, chopped
1 bunch fresh thyme, chopped
3 tablespoons hoisin sauce
3 tablespoons barbecue sauce (optional)
2 tablespoons honey
2 small onions, roughly chopped,
plus 1 small onion, sliced
6 garlic cloves, chopped
8 pork chops, about 175g each
2 plum tomatoes, chopped
¼ pepper, sliced
1 tablespoon chopped fresh mint
240ml water

Method

1 Mix together the orange zest and juice, ginger, soy sauce, coriander, thyme, 2 tablespoons of the hoisin sauce, the barbecue sauce, if using, 1 tablespoon of the honey, the chopped onions and garlic in a small bowl. Place the pork chops in a baking dish and pour the marinade over the chops, making sure it covers them well. Leave to marinate in the fridge for at least 4 hours.

2 Preheat the oven to 200°C/gas mark 6.

3 Transfer the chops and marinade to a flameproof roasting tin, arrange the chops in a single layer and roast for 40–50 minutes, turning the chops over halfway through, until the pork is cooked through and soft.

4 Transfer the pan with the pork chops and marinade (now enriched with pan juices) to the hob over a medium heat. Add the tomatoes, sliced onion, pepper, mint and water over and around the chops and mix into the marinade. Stir in the remaining 1 tablespoon each of honey and hoisin sauce and bring to the boil. Reduce the heat to low, cover the pan with foil and simmer for 20 minutes. The chops will be juicy, soft and tasty after cooking in their own liquid. Serve hot.

MARMALADE-GLAZED LEG OF LAMB

Leg of lamb is a favourite of ours and brings back many childhood memories of our summers in England with Aunt Winsome. Many Sundays were spent lunching in the English countryside on lamb, roast potatoes, mint sauce and stolen sips of Pimm's! Instead of the traditional leg of lamb with mint sauce or jelly, we add a touch of fresh ginger and Scotch bonnet to the marinade and baste the lamb with a marmalade glaze. Feel free to serve a jelly of some sort on the side as well, or just drizzle a little of the marmalade glaze over the carved meat. Delish!

Serves 6–8

2 garlic cloves, very finely chopped
½ Scotch bonnet chilli, very finely chopped
1 tablespoon grated orange zest
2 teaspoons fresh chopped sage
1 tablespoon chopped fresh thyme
2 teaspoons peeled and grated fresh ginger
2 tablespoons soy sauce
60ml extra virgin olive oil
2 tablespoons Appleton Estate V/X rum
(or any dark rum)
sea salt and freshly ground pepper
boneless leg of lamb joint, 1.8kg

For the Rum and Marmalade Glaze

(MAKES ABOUT 300g)
160g orange marmalade
120ml orange juice
2 teaspoons brown sugar
2 tablespoons chopped fresh thyme
60ml Appleton Estate V/X Rum
(or any dark rum)

Method

1 Put the garlic, Scotch bonnet, orange zest, sage, thyme, ginger, soy sauce, oil and rum in a medium bowl and whisk until blended. Season with salt and pepper. Place the leg of lamb in a baking dish and pour the marinade over the lamb, working it into the meat with your hands. Refrigerate for a minimum of 3 hours.

2 Allow the lamb to come to room temperature before roasting. Preheat the oven to 180°C/gas mark 4.

3 To make the rum and marmalade glaze, combine the marmalade, orange juice, brown sugar and thyme in a small saucepan. Simmer over a medium heat for about 10 minutes until syrupy, then whisk in the rum and simmer for a further minute.

4 Roast the lamb for 1–1½ hours, depending on the size of the leg, repeatedly basting with the marmalade glaze. For medium doneness, an instant-read thermometer inserted into the thickest part of the leg should register 60–63°C. Leave the lamb to rest for 5–10 minutes before carving and serving.

HYACINTH'S POT ROAST

Hyacinth, who has worked with us for a very long time, has a stable of go-to recipes. This is one of our favourites. We like to serve this with rice and peas (page 142), fried ripe plantains and whatever seasonal root vegetables are on hand. The Cho Cho Packets (page 132) would also go very well with it.

Serves 6

3 tablespoons mixed herbs (such as mint, basil, thyme and rosemary), chopped

1 bunch spring onions, chopped

1 onion, finely chopped, plus 1 onion, chopped

½ Scotch bonnet chilli, deseeded and finely chopped, plus 1 whole

2 teaspoons sea salt, plus more for seasoning

2 teaspoons freshly ground black pepper, plus more for seasoning

2.5cm fresh ginger, peeled and grated

6 garlic cloves, very finely chopped, plus 8 whole, peeled

1 tablespoon olive oil

1 tablespoon soy sauce

beef shoulder joint, 2.25kg, trimmed

3 tablespoons vegetable oil

1 carrot, peeled and chopped

2 plum tomatoes, diced

1 bunch fresh thyme, chopped, plus more for seasoning

60ml white wine (optional)

1 teaspoon sugar, or more to taste

1 teaspoon cornflour mixed to a paste with 1 tablespoon cold water (optional)

Method

1 Mix together the herbs, spring onions, finely chopped onion, chopped Scotch bonnet, salt, pepper, ginger, finely chopped garlic, olive oil and soy sauce in a small bowl. Using a sharp knife, score small holes in the roast and stuff the marinade in the holes, then rub the remaining marinade all over the outside of the meat. If the roast is loose, tie it together with kitchen string to make it easier to carve later. Place in a baking dish and leave to stand in the fridge for at least 2 hours.

2 Heat the vegetable oil in a large flameproof casserole dish over a medium-high heat. Wipe off any excess marinade from the meat and sear on all sides until browned. Add a touch of water, cover the pan and cook over a low heat for about 30 minutes. Keep adding water a little at a time as the existing water evaporates. Don't add a lot of water at once; we want the meat to make its own flavourful gravy.

3 After 30 minutes, add the carrot, tomatoes, chopped onion, garlic cloves, thyme and whole Scotch bonnet to the pan. (Be careful not to burst the pepper, as we want the Scotch bonnet flavour without its interior heat.) Keep adding water, a little at a time, for about 20 minutes until the meat is cooked through.

4 Transfer the meat to a chopping board and leave to rest. Return the dish with the pan juices and vegetables to the hob over a medium heat. Adjust the seasoning of the gravy with the white wine, if using, and more thyme, salt, pepper and sugar as needed. If you want to thicken the gravy, whisk in the cornflour paste.

5 Carve the roast, transfer to a platter and pour the gravy over the meat, reserving some gravy to serve on the side.

COUNTRY-STYLE SHEPHERD'S PIE

Shepherd's pie is the ultimate comfort food. 'Mince', or cooked minced beef, reminds us of our grandmother, MaMa, as she would always cook it for us when we came home for school break. This updated version incorporates both sweet potato and white potato: a layer of mashed sweet potato at the base is covered with beef mince and then topped with a layer of regular mashed potatoes. It's a yummy one-pot meal that is sure to please.

Serves 6–8

4 tablespoons soy sauce, plus more
if necessary
2 bunches fresh thyme, chopped
4 garlic cloves, chopped, plus 3 garlic cloves,
finely chopped
½ Scotch bonnet chilli, very finely chopped,
plus ½ teaspoon very finely chopped
2 teaspoons sea salt, plus more for seasoning
1.3kg beef mince
900g white potatoes, peeled and cubed
900g sweet potatoes, peeled and cubed
30g salted butter, plus more for greasing
60g Cheddar cheese, grated
120ml full-fat milk
freshly ground white pepper
1 tablespoon olive oil
1 onion, finely chopped
1 carrot, peeled and diced
1 pepper, diced
2 plum tomatoes, chopped
1 teaspoon tomato purée
60ml white wine
25g Parmesan cheese, freshly grated

Method

1 Whisk together 2 tablespoons of the soy sauce, half the thyme, the chopped garlic, the ½ finely chopped Scotch bonnet and salt in a large bowl. Add the mince, toss to coat and set aside.

2 Meanwhile, put a large saucepan of salted water on to boil. First add the white potatoes and cook for 20 minutes. Using a slotted spoon, transfer to a plate. Add the sweet potatoes to the same pan and boil for about 20 minutes until cooked through.

3 While the sweet potatoes are boiling, mash the white potatoes with half the butter, half the Cheddar and half the milk. Season with salt and white pepper and set aside. Drain and transfer the sweet potato to a plate, then mash with the remaining butter, Cheddar and milk. Season with salt and pepper again and set aside.

4 Preheat the oven to 190°C/gas mark 5.

5 Heat the oil in a sauté pan over a medium heat. Add the onion, the finely chopped garlic, the ½ teaspoon finely chopped Scotch bonnet, the carrot, pepper and remaining thyme and sauté for about 5 minutes until softened. Add the marinated beef and sauté, breaking up the mince with a spatula, for 10 minutes. Stir in the remaining 2 tablespoons soy sauce, the tomatoes, tomato purée and white wine and cook until the tomatoes break down and much of the liquid has evaporated. Season with salt and pepper.

6 Brush the base of a baking dish with butter and pack the mashed sweet potato in the bottom of the dish. Top with a layer of the beef mixture and cover with a layer of the mashed potatoes. Sprinkle with the Parmesan and bake for 20 minutes or until golden brown. Leave to cool for 10 minutes before serving.

ROAST SALMON WITH CITRUS GINGER AÏOLI

This is the easiest and quickest 'Sunday roast' you will ever cook. Roast salmon makes for a much lighter version of your typical Sunday meal – and, hey, who says your roast has to be meat? Salmon is not indigenous to the Caribbean but works surprisingly well when infused with Caribbean flavours like ginger and citrus.

Serves 4–6

3 tablespoons olive oil
juice of 1 orange
juice of 1 lime
1 bunch fresh rosemary, chopped
2.5cm fresh ginger, peeled and grated
4 garlic cloves
sea salt and freshly ground black pepper
side of salmon, skin on, 900g–1.1kg
2 oranges, thinly sliced

For the Citrus Ginger Aïoli

juice and grated zest of 1 orange
225g mayonnaise
1 teaspoon Dijon mustard
2 tablespoons olive oil
1 teaspoon very finely chopped garlic
1 teaspoon peeled and grated fresh ginger
sea salt and freshly ground black pepper

Method

1 Preheat the oven to 260°C, or 240°C/gas mark 9 if that's the highest setting you have.

2 Mix together the oil, orange and lime juices, rosemary, ginger and garlic in a small bowl, and season with salt and pepper. Place the salmon in a large baking dish and pour the marinade on top. Arrange the orange slices on top of the salmon. Leave to marinate in the fridge for about 1 hour.

3 To make the citrus ginger aïoli, simply whisk together the orange juice and zest, mayonnaise, mustard, oil, garlic and ginger in a small bowl until well combined. Season with salt and pepper. Cover the bowl with clingfilm and refrigerate.

4 Transfer the salmon, skin side down, to a large, shallow roasting tin and roast for 15 minutes. Reduce the oven temperature to 220°C/gas mark 7 and roast for 5–10 minutes until cooked through (the salmon flesh should be flaky but still moist).

5 Transfer the whole side of salmon to a platter and serve hot or at room temperature, drizzled with some of the aïoli. Serve with the roasted orange slices and the remaining aïoli on the side.

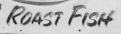

"...K PORK" "JERK CHICKEN" "ROAST FISH"

STEAM
FRY CHIC...
STEW CHIC...
FRY FISH

...LOSSOM...

...AST FOOD

6

OXTAIL, MY ASS!

THE CLASSICS, REVISTED

No Caribbean cookbook would be complete without recipes for some of the more traditional stews and one-pot dishes found throughout the region. In this chapter, we share our versions of some good old-fashioned home cooking, with our own special twists, like adding fresh mango, white rum and coconut milk to our curry goat.

The best cooks in the Caribbean are the home cooks, mostly women, who spend a good portion of their time creating and serving meals for their families. They make home that special place where the kitchen is filled with the aroma of tasty dishes like the ones in this chapter, which welcome friends and strangers alike, the minute they cross the threshold.

MUMMY'S 'CHINESE' CHICKEN WITH ORANGE, GINGER AND RUM

Our mother makes this wonderful unique chicken dish; it's a really nice change from the typical stewed chicken or fricassee chicken that we make in so many of the islands. We love the Asian influences combined with the island rum and the citrus.

Serves 6

3 tablespoons soy sauce
5cm fresh ginger, peeled and grated
6 garlic cloves, chopped
freshly ground black pepper
1 whole chicken, 1.8kg, cut in half
60ml vegetable, groundnut or sesame oil
60ml mushroom soy sauce
240ml water
1 teaspoon grated orange zest, or more to taste
2 tablespoons brown sugar, or more to taste
2 tablespoons rum, or more to taste
5 star anise
1 spring onion, sliced, for garnish
fresh coriander, for garnish

Method

1 Mix together the soy sauce, half the ginger, half the garlic and a generous grind of pepper in a baking dish. Add the chicken halves, toss well and leave to marinate in the fridge for at least 30 minutes.

2 Heat the oil in a medium saucepan over a medium-high heat until very hot. Place the chicken halves in the pan, skin side down, and sear. Turn the chicken over to sear the other side. Mix the soy sauce with the water and pour it over the chicken. Add the remaining ginger and garlic and bring to the boil, then reduce the heat and simmer for 20 minutes. Add the orange zest, brown sugar, rum and star anise and then simmer for a further 8–10 minutes until the sauce is thickened and the chicken is cooked through.

3 Transfer the chicken to a chopping board and leave to cool, then chop into bite-sized pieces. Adjust the seasoning of the sauce with more sugar, zest or rum as necessary, and cook for about another 5 minutes to reduce and thicken a bit more.

4 Divide the chicken between serving plates, pour the sauce over the chicken and garnish with the spring onion and coriander.

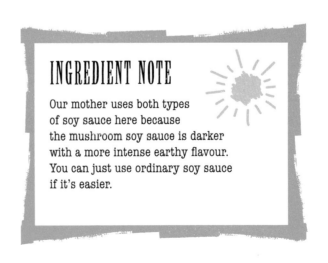

INGREDIENT NOTE

Our mother uses both types of soy sauce here because the mushroom soy sauce is darker with a more intense earthy flavour. You can just use ordinary soy sauce if it's easier.

OXTAIL WITH BROAD BEANS

If there is one item that we would consider 'hungry belly' food, it would be oxtail, the singular favourite dish of many a Jamaican man far and wide. The oxtails are simmered down in a thick, rich gravy with broad beans, spinners (or flour dumplings) and vegetables, and served over a mound of rice and peas. In this version, we use a technique we learnt from a former employee, Daphne, that makes supremely tender oxtails and delicious gravy: use ice rather than water to create the cooking liquid for the oxtail, adding more ice a little at a time as the water evaporates. Alternatively, you can simply use water (adding a little at a time) or cook the oxtails in a pressure cooker, which shortens the cooking time.

Serves 6

1 onion, chopped
3 spring onions, sliced, plus 1 bunch spring onions, roughly chopped
8 garlic cloves, chopped
½ Scotch bonnet chilli, deseeded and chopped, plus 1 whole (optional)
120ml water
1.3kg oxtails, trimmed
2 tablespoons soy sauce, plus more to taste
2 teaspoons sea salt, plus more for seasoning
1 teaspoon freshly ground black pepper, plus more for seasoning
1 bunch fresh thyme leaves, chopped, plus 1 bunch thyme sprigs
4 tablespoons vegetable oil
3 x 300g cans broad beans, drained

For the Spinners

190g plain flour
pinch of sea salt
120ml water

Method

1 Combine half the onion, the 3 sliced spring onions, half the garlic and the chopped Scotch bonnet with the water in a medium bowl. Rub the oxtails with 1 tablespoon of the soy sauce, salt, pepper and chopped thyme in a baking dish. Pour the seasoning ingredients over the oxtails and leave to marinate in the fridge for 24 hours to flavour and tenderise the meat.

2 Heat 2 tablespoons of the oil in a deep saucepan over a high heat. Working in batches, place a single layer of oxtails in the pan and cook them for about 5 minutes per side until browned. Transfer the browned meat to a plate and set aside. Add a little more oil only if necessary, as the fat rendered from the meat will give you additional oil, and repeat with the rest of the oxtails in batches, which will take about 30 minutes in total.

3 Add about 250ml water to the pan juices, scrape up the browned bits from the base of the pan and pour into a bowl, then set aside. Return the oxtails to the pan, add the remaining onion, the chopped spring onions, remaining garlic, the thyme sprigs, the whole Scotch bonnet, if using, and the remaining 1 tablespoon soy sauce and sauté for about 5 minutes over a high heat, making sure the oxtail is well coated. Cover the meat with a layer of ice, cover the pan and simmer the meat.

4 After about 40 minutes, return the pan juices to the pan and cook the oxtails slowly over a medium to medium-high heat. Keep adding ice, a little at a time, making sure there is just enough liquid to cover the meat, and cook for about 2 hours until the oxtails are tender and cooked through (you can also use water in lieu of ice).

5 Meanwhile, make the spinners. Mix together the flour and salt in a small bowl. Add the water and knead until a dough forms. Shape the dough into a ball and leave it to rest for at least 15 minutes.

6 After the meat has been cooking for about 2 hours, take small pieces of dough, roll them into 'cigarettes' and place them directly in the simmering liquid in the pan. Add the broad beans and simmer for another 30 minutes or so until the liquid is thick. Taste and adjust the seasoning, then serve.

CURRIED GOAT WITH WHITE RUM AND FRESH MANGO

Everyone in Jamaica loves 'a curry goat'. In fact, many festive occasions as well as funerals and wakes are commemorated with the slaughter of a goat as a blessing, as it is a widely held local superstition that the letting of blood wards away evil spirits and protects the living. The goat meat is cooked down in a Dutch oven or 'dutchie' over an outdoor flame for many hours. The remaining parts of the goat are never wasted; they're used to make a hearty soup called Mannish Water. Even the goat's testicles are included, as they are supposed to give added virility and stamina to the males who drink it. (We think this is an acquired taste and can't pretend we are fans.) In our version, we modernise curry goat a bit by adding some fresh mango, white rum and coconut milk, and serve it up with a fresh banana raisin salsa, toasted grated coconut, toasted peanuts and cashews, rice and shop-bought roti.

Serves 6–8

Banana Raisin Salsa
4 medium ripe bananas, diced
40g raisins
2 tablespoons finely diced red onion
2 tablespoons chopped fresh coriander
1 tablespoon fresh lime juice
1 tablespoon chopped fresh mint

1 large onion, finely chopped
7 spring onions, finely chopped
8 garlic cloves, finely chopped
2.5cm fresh ginger, peeled and finely chopped
1 Scotch bonnet chilli, finely chopped
4 tablespoons curry powder
180ml vegetable oil, plus 1 tablespoon
1 bunch fresh thyme
sea salt and freshly ground black pepper
1.6kg boneless goat (or lamb) meat, cut into 2.5cm pieces
about 950ml water
1 x 400ml can coconut milk
60ml white rum
12 whole allspice berries
2 carrots (about 450g), peeled and diced
1 potato (about 225g), peeled and diced
85g stoned and peeled mango, diced

Method

1 To make the banana raisin salsa, combine all the ingredients in a bowl and leave to stand for at least 2 hours until the flavours blend.

2 Mix together the onion, spring onions, garlic, ginger and Scotch bonnet in a large bowl. Transfer half the onion mixture to a baking dish and add 3 tablespoons of the curry powder, the 1 tablespoon oil, the thyme, 1 tablespoon salt and 1 teaspoon pepper. Add the goat meat, toss to coat the meat with the spice mixture and leave to marinate for at least 30 minutes.

3 Heat 2 tablespoons oil in a large saucepan over a medium-high heat. Sear the goat in batches to avoid overcrowding the pan, then transfer to a bowl and set aside. Deglaze the pan with a little water to get all the scrapings from the base of the pan, and then pour over the seared meat.

4 In the same pan, heat another 2 tablespoons oil and add the remaining 1 tablespoon curry powder to toast the curry for about 1 minute. Add the remaining onion mixture and cook for about 2 minutes, then stir in the seared goat meat and cooking liquid. Add the water (or just enough to cover the goat meat) and bring to the boil. Cook over a high heat for about 40 minutes.

5 Add the coconut milk, rum and allspice to the pan and cook for another 15 minutes, adding more liquid as needed. Add the carrots, potato and mango and cook for about another 35 minutes until the meat is tender.

6 Divide the goat, vegetables and mango between individual bowls and pour over the sauce. Serve with the salsa, along with the array of condiments noted above.

TRINIDADIAN CHICKEN AND RICE (PELAU)

Pelau will always remind us of our time living in Trinidad. This one-pot dish of chicken, rice, gungo (pigeon) peas, coconut milk and vegetables is so good that you will keep eating it for days after it is made. This recipe calls for the quintessential 'green seasoning' that is the basis of all Trini cooking; this amazing seasoning blend can be used as a marinade for many meats and as a flavour enhancer for many dishes. This delicious recipe comes courtesy of our Trini friend Cree, who has saved our lives with her incredible pelau on many occasions during Trinidad Carnival, when we roll in exhausted from a night of debaucherous behaviour – and one too many glasses of rum. Thanks, Cree.

Serves 12

For the Trini-Style Green Seasoning

4 spring onions, chopped
1 bunch fresh thyme
2 bunches fresh chadon beni (culantro) or coriander
1 bunch fresh parsley
12 garlic cloves, peeled
1 large onion, roughly chopped
1 Scotch bonnet chilli (optional)
6 canned pimiento peppers or jarred piquillo peppers, drained
3 tablespoons distilled white vinegar
3 tablespoons vegetable oil
sea salt and freshly ground black pepper

1 tablespoon soy sauce
1 teaspoon tomato ketchup
3 tablespoons vegetable oil
sea salt and freshly ground black pepper
1 whole chicken, 1.3kg, jointed
400g dried gungo (pigeon) peas, soaked overnight
3 tablespoons brown sugar
475ml canned coconut milk
375g easy-cook white long-grain rice, washed and drained
100g onions, chopped
115g peeled and deseeded calabaza pumpkin or other starchy squash, such as butternut, chopped
65g peeled carrots, chopped
1 whole Scotch bonnet chilli
50g spring onion, sliced

Method

1 To make the Trini-style green seasoning, purée the spring onions, thyme, chadon beni or coriander, parsley, garlic, onion, Scotch bonnet, if using, peppers, vinegar and oil in a blender. Remove to a baking dish and season with salt and pepper.

2 Add the soy sauce, ketchup and 1 tablespoon of the oil to the green seasoning. Season with salt and pepper, add the chicken and set aside while you cook the peas.

3 Cover the peas with salted water in a small saucepan and bring to the boil. Reduce the heat to medium-low and simmer for 30–35 minutes until the peas are cooked. Drain the peas and reserve the cooking liquid.

4 Heat the remaining 2 tablespoons oil in a saucepan over a medium heat. When the oil is hot, sprinkle the brown sugar evenly over the base of the pan. Let the sugar melt, and when it starts to bubble, add the chicken and sear it, turning often, for about 8 minutes until browned and coated with the 'burnt' sugar. Add the peas and stir. Add 250ml of the reserved cooking liquid and the coconut milk and cook for about 30 minutes.

5 Stir in the rice and up to another 250ml of the reserved cooking liquid as needed and bring to the boil. Cook for about 5 minutes, then add the onions, pumpkin or other squash, carrots and whole Scotch bonnet. Season with salt and pepper and simmer for about 15 minutes until much of the liquid has evaporated. Cover the pan and cook for 30–40 minutes until all the liquid has evaporated.

6 Serve garnished with the spring onion.

JERKED PORK WITH MANGO GINGER SAUCE

If there is one dish that Jamaica is well known for, it is jerk. Our jerk seasoning is delicious and spicy enough to make you stand up and say HEY! It's the real deal, not tempered down in any way, so be warned: if you can't take the heat, stay away from the jerk! For a unique kick, we add a little coffee. Also bear in mind that Scotch bonnet chillies in Jamaica are much more spicy than other chillies available overseas, so feel free to add more if you want to 'kick it up' a notch. For a more refined version of this dish, we use pork fillet – simply barbecue it (you'll need a barbecue/stove-top smoker), carve it, cover it with mango ginger sauce and pop in the oven for 10 minutes, although this last step is totally up to you. We like to serve this with roasted yam and roasted ripe plantains, and Creole-Spiced Slaw (page 135).

Serves 10

For Our Special Super-Spicy Coffee Jerk Seasoning
(Makes about 600ml)
12 Scotch bonnet chillies
120ml vegetable oil
240ml coconut oil
1 tablespoon molasses
1 bunch spring onions, chopped
2 large garlic cloves, chopped
20g fresh thyme, chopped
pinch of sea salt
3 tablespoons allspice berries, crushed
3 tablespoons peeled and chopped fresh ginger
½ teaspoon ground cinnamon
dash of freshly grated nutmeg
1 teaspoon ground coriander
2 tablespoons red rum
2 tablespoons distilled white vinegar
60ml brewed coffee

boneless pork shoulder joint, 2.25kg
(or 1 whole pork fillet, 1.8kg)
sea salt

For the Mango Ginger Sauce
330g stoned and peeled mango, chopped
1 tablespoon peeled and very finely chopped fresh ginger
2 tablespoons fresh lime juice
240ml mango juice
2 tablespoons brown sugar
sea salt and freshly ground black pepper

Method

1 To make the jerk seasoning, blend all the ingredients in a blender until smooth. Rub the outside of the pork with salt and place it in a baking dish. Cover with the jerk seasoning and leave to marinate for at least 24 hours.

2 To make the sauce, combine all the ingredients except seasoning in a small saucepan over a medium heat and simmer for 10 minutes. Transfer to a blender and purée until very smooth. Season with salt and pepper.

3 Cook the pork on a gas or charcoal barbecue on an open medium flame with a barbecue/stove-top smoker, turning from time to time, for 2 hours or until an instant-read thermometer inserted into the thickest part of the meat registers 63°C and the outside is dark and charred. Alternatively, preheat the oven to 260°C, or 240°C/gas mark 9 if that's the highest setting you have, and roast the pork for 1 hour 40 minutes. Transfer the pork to a chopping board and chop into 2.5cm pieces. If using pork fillet, it will cook within 15–20 minutes; carve it into slices about 5mm thick.

4 Preheat the oven, if necessary, to 230°C/gas mark 8. Place the pork in a roasting tin, ladle some mango ginger sauce over and roast for 10 minutes for the glaze to set. Serve hot, with the remaining sauce on the side.

BLUE MOUNTAIN BEEF STEW WITH STOUT

In Jamaica, 'stew beef' is a popular lunch item, often served with rice and peas. In this version, we add Jamaican stout and coffee, and braise the beef instead of stewing it over the fire as is traditional. It comes out a bit more like a beef bourguignon, which we happen to love; the stout, however, adds a much more intense flavour than red wine.

Serves 6-8

1 teaspoon dried rosemary
2 bunches fresh thyme, chopped
8 garlic cloves, chopped
1cm fresh ginger, peeled and grated
½ Scotch bonnet chilli, deseeded and very finely chopped
1 teaspoon sea salt, plus more for seasoning
1 teaspoon freshly ground black pepper, plus more for seasoning
2 tablespoons brewed coffee, plus 60ml, preferably Blue Mountain
1 tablespoon soy sauce
1.1kg braising steak
120ml olive oil
65–95g plain flour
2 carrots, peeled and chopped
1 onion, chopped
2 tablespoons tomato purée
2 bay leaves
120ml Dragon stout
475ml water
1 teaspoon sugar (optional)

Method

1 Preheat the oven to 160°C/gas mark 3.

2 Stir together the rosemary, half the thyme and garlic, the ginger, Scotch bonnet, salt, pepper, the 2 tablespoons coffee and soy sauce in a small bowl. Season the beef well with salt and pepper, then rub the marinade all over the meat.

3 Heat the oil in a large flameproof casserole dish over a medium-high heat. Dust the beef with the flour and fry quickly in batches to brown. Transfer to a plate lined with kitchen paper and set aside.

4 Add the carrots, onion and the remaining garlic to the pan and sauté over a medium heat until browned. Add the tomato purée and cook for 5 minutes. Add the bay leaves and remaining thyme.

5 Return the meat to the pan and add the stout. Cook for 10–15 minutes until reduced, then add the water and the remaining 60ml coffee and bring to the boil. Once boiling, cover the pan and place in the oven for about 2 hours until the meat is tender.

6 Transfer the meat and vegetables to a deep serving dish. Skim off any excess fat from the cooking liquid and return to the hob. Reduce for 10 minutes over a medium heat until thickened. Taste and adjust the seasoning with the sugar, if necessary. Pour the sauce over the meat and vegetables and serve.

GUYANESE PEPPERPOT

Pepperpot is Guyana's national dish – not to be confused with Jamaican pepperpot, which is a soup made from callaloo and coconut milk. Guyanese pepperpot is a stew made from all kinds of meats that are cooked down in cassareep (a sort of syrup made from cassava). Traditionally eaten on Christmas morning with a special plait bread, we often ate this stew while living in Trinidad, as we had great family friends who were Guyanese. We have since developed such a love for the flavour of cassareep that it always has a place in our storecupboard (see page 16). Cassareep may be difficult to find, but if you see it in a Caribbean market, make sure you buy some and try this delectable stew. Traditional pepperpot flavours the meats with orange peel, cinnamon, brown sugar and cloves. In our version, we season oxtail and braising pork and/or beef with thyme and garlic. Feel free to add in some of the traditional seasonings mentioned above, and use whatever combination of meats you desire.

Serves 8–10

½ Scotch bonnet chilli, deseeded and very finely chopped, plus 1 whole
1 head garlic, cloves peeled but left whole, plus 4 cloves, chopped
3 onions, chopped
1 teaspoon soy sauce
1 tablespoon vegetable oil, plus 60ml
sea salt and freshly ground black pepper
2.25kg oxtails
2.25kg boneless pork shoulder or braising steak, or a mixture of both, cubed
55g brown sugar
2 bunches spring onions, chopped
1 tablespoon chopped fresh thyme
1.1 litres cassareep
600ml water
chopped fresh parsley, for garnish
cooked rice or hardo bread, for serving

COOKING HINT

If cassareep is not available, you can still make a nice stew by adding a splash of molasses and soy sauce after caramelising the sugar.

Method

1 Combine the finely chopped Scotch bonnet, whole garlic cloves, a third of the onions, the soy sauce and the 1 tablespoon oil in a large baking dish and season with salt and pepper. Add the meat, mix well and leave to marinate in the fridge for at least 24 hours.

2 Heat the remaining 60ml oil in a large saucepan over a medium heat. Add the brown sugar and cook until the sugar is caramelised – don't allow it to burn! Add the pork and sear to seal in the flavours. Transfer to a plate and set aside. Add the oxtail to the pot and sear in batches to brown it. Return all the oxtail to the pan and add the 4 chopped garlic cloves, the remaining onion, the spring onions, whole Scotch bonnet and thyme. Stir well and cook for about 5 minutes.

3 Meanwhile, mix the cassareep with the water in a medium bowl. Gradually add the cassareep liquid, a little at a time, until the meat is covered (you won't use it all – reserve the leftovers). Bring to the boil, then reduce the heat, cover and simmer for 30 minutes.

4 Return the pork to the pan and add some more cassareep liquid. Cook over a low heat, stirring occasionally and gradually adding more cassareep liquid as the liquid in the pot evaporates, for about 2 hours. Slow cooking is needed to tenderise the meat and infuse the flavours. The meat should always be just covered with liquid – don't add too much. Once the meat is tender and cooked through, the gravy should be nice and thick and rich.

5 Taste to adjust the seasoning, garnish with parsley and serve with rice or hardo bread.

SPICY GARLIC 'PEPPER' PRAWNS

Pepper 'swims', or prawns seasoned with chilli peppers, are sold by 'shrimp' vendors on the roadside and at traffic lights in various parts of the island. Served at room temperature out of little plastic bags, they make for a tasty, quick, 'smoke out of the ears' snack when journeying around Jamaica. Middle Quarters, in the parish of St Elizabeth on the south coast, is particularly well known for its pepper swims. This is our version, which we serve hot as a main dish, with our coconut rice pilaf (page 141).

Serves 4–6

450g fresh or thawed frozen raw large king prawns (16–20), in shells with heads on
2 tablespoons sea salt
475ml vegetable oil
1 Scotch bonnet chilli, chopped with seeds
6 garlic cloves, diced
25g spring onion, sliced
1 teaspoon sugar

Method

1 Butterfly the prawns and remove the veins but leave the shells and heads on. Place in a bowl and rub the prawns with 1 tablespoon of the salt, then leave to stand for at least 30 minutes.

2 Heat the oil in a wok or frying pan over a medium-high heat. Add the prawns in batches and deep-fry for 40–60 seconds, then quickly remove from the oil with a slotted spoon and drain on kitchen paper. When all the prawns have been deep-fried, pour the oil out of the pan, leaving just 1 tablespoon.

3 Quickly sauté the Scotch bonnet, garlic, spring onions, sugar and remaining 1 tablespoon sea salt in small batches over a high heat for a few seconds. Add the prawns in batches, give them a quick toss to coat with the seasoning and remove quickly from the pan. Repeat until all the prawns are finished. Serve immediately.

WHOLE ROAST SNAPPER WITH GRILLED LIME AND MOJITO OIL

Traditional roast fish in Jamaica is roasted in a foil parcel with pumpkin, okra, Scotch bonnet and seasonings. We love fresh fish with a sea salty, crispy skin, so we roast this in a high oven to get it nice and charred. The mojito oil is drizzled all over the finished fish, which we serve with grilled limes – it's fresh, clean and just divine!

Serves 4

For the Mint Lime Mojito Oil
(Makes about 475ml)
45g loosely packed fresh mint leaves
25g fresh parsley leaves, finely chopped
2 garlic cloves, chopped
2 teaspoons sugar
2 teaspoons grated lime zest
1 teaspoon sea salt
½ teaspoon Scotch bonnet chilli, deseeded and very finely chopped
250ml olive oil
3 tablespoons fresh lime juice
2 tablespoons capers, chopped (optional)
1 teaspoon freshly ground black pepper

4 fresh whole red snapper, gutted and scaled, 450g each
4 teaspoons fresh lime juice
2 tablespoons olive oil
1 bunch fresh coriander, chopped
1 tablespoon peeled and grated fresh ginger
1 tablespoon sea salt
1 bunch fresh sprigs of thyme
1 lime, thinly sliced
2–3 slivers Scotch bonnet chilli (optional)
freshly ground black pepper
4 limes and/or lemons, halved

Method

1 To make the mint lime mojito oil, using a mortar and pestle, muddle the mint and parsley with the garlic, sugar, lime zest, salt and finely chopped Scotch bonnet. Transfer to a small bowl and add the oil, lime juice, capers, if using, and pepper. Leave the oil to stand in the fridge for a minimum of 6 hours.

2 Rub each fish with 1 teaspoon lime juice. Mix together the oil, coriander, ginger and salt in a small bowl. Score the outside of the fish with three cuts on either side and massage the marinade into the skin, the cuts and inside the cavity of the fish. Stuff each cavity with thyme sprigs, lime slices and slivers of Scotch bonnet, if using. Generously sprinkle the outside of the fish with sea salt and pepper and leave to rest for 1 hour.

3 Preheat the oven to 230°C/gas mark 8. Roast the fish for 20 minutes until the skin is slightly charred.

4 Place the limes and/or lemons directly on the oven shelf, cut sides down, until marked and slightly softened.

5 Place each fish on a serving plate and drizzle generously with the mojito oil. Garnish with the limes and/or lemons to squeeze onto the fish to add an incredible kick!

AL FRESCO CARIBBEAN

GRILL PAN AND COAL POT COOKING

In the Caribbean, we are blessed with blazingly hot days and warm, sultry nights year round. We live outdoors; we eat and drink outdoors and, while we do enjoy our homes, we love to socialise under the sun and stars. In this chapter, we share some of the most popular dishes from our off-site event menus, when we often had very little equipment to work with and were working in remote and challenging venues (like the middle of the race-course track or on a remote beach or mountain top) with no electricity, no running water and very few facilities. With our paltry equipment budget, we were compelled to develop a series of recipes around the coal pot and jerk pan, which soon became our signature, allowing us to cook fresh on site and retain authentic island flavour in our many dishes.

Many classic island recipes are traditionally prepared outdoors on a coal pot or in a griddle pan. It's common to see roadside chefs selling their specialities any time of day or night on any Caribbean island – whether it's pan chicken, jerk pork, shark and bake, doubles or corn soup, the food is always hot and always divine. We consider these recipes to be more contemporary and cleaner versions of the traditional al fresco preparations that can be found in the islands. So stoke up your barbie and give them a go. *Bon appétit*!

PIMENTO-CRUSTED BEEF TENDERLOIN WITH ISLAND CHIMICHURRI

This recipe is a stripped-down version of jerk – we separate the elements that go into jerk seasoning and recombine them with this mouthwatering version of beef fillet. The beef is crusted with allspice berries (pimento), similar to beef *au poivre*, and grilled on a traditional coal pan. When ready, it is drizzled with Scotch bonnet oil and garnished with chargrilled spring onions. A West Indian version of chimichurri made with culantro, Scotch bonnet and lime rounds this dish off nicely. We served this up family style at a beautiful colonial house in the hills of Hanover for a rehearsal dinner organised, designed and executed by Los Angeles-based event planner to the stars Yifat Oren. It was the single most spectacular event that we have ever seen, executed or had the pleasure to work on; luckily for us, the food was a hit!

Serves 8–10

35g whole black peppercorns
70g allspice berries
1 whole beef fillet, 1.8–2.7kg
300ml olive oil
½ tablespoon sea salt, plus more
for seasoning
4 garlic cloves, very finely chopped, plus
1 tablespoon chopped
1 bunch fresh thyme, chopped, plus
2 tablespoons chopped
1 red onion, thickly sliced
6 portobello mushrooms, caps only, sliced
3 bunches spring onions
drizzle of Scotch Bonnet Oil, or more
to taste (page 46)

For the Caribbean Chimichurri

50g fresh parsley, chopped
40g fresh coriander, chopped
20g fresh chadon beni (culantro), chopped
(if not available, use 60g fresh coriander in
total, chopped)
20g fresh mint, chopped
60ml fresh lime juice
½ teaspoon very finely chopped Scotch
bonnet chilli
5 garlic cloves, chopped
1 bay leaf
1 tablespoon sea salt
350ml olive oil
½ teaspoon brown sugar

Method

1 Place the peppercorns and allspice on the bottom half of a tea towel. Fold over the top half of the towel and crush the peppercorns and allspice seeds together by rolling over them with a bottle.

2 Rub the beef with 250ml of the oil, the salt, the 4 finely chopped garlic cloves and the chopped bunch of thyme, making sure the beef is well salted. Roll the beef in the crushed pepper and allspice mixture to coat and press the pepper and allspice into the surface of the beef. Refrigerate for at least 2 hours.

3 To make the Caribbean chimichurri, put the parsley, coriander, chadon beni, mint, lime juice, Scotch bonnet, garlic, bay leaf, sea salt, oil and brown sugar in a food processor and process until well blended.

4 Heat up a gas or charcoal barbecue or a griddle pan over a high heat. Combine the remaining 50ml oil, 2 tablespoons chopped thyme and 1 tablespoon chopped garlic in a small bowl. Season with salt, add the red onion and mushrooms and mix well. Chargrill the onions and mushrooms for about 10 minutes in total, then transfer to a plate and keep warm in the oven.

5 Add the beef to the barbecue or griddle pan and cook to the desired doneness – about 15 minutes for medium. Transfer to a chopping board and leave to rest before carving. Place the spring onions on the barbecue or in the griddle pan for about 1 minute until marked.

6 Carve the beef and place on a platter, garnished with the chargrilled scallions, onions and mushrooms. Drizzle the chimichurri and the Scotch bonnet oil over the beef; serve the remaining chimichurri on the side.

BARBECUED LOBSTER WITH CHILLI LIME BUTTER AND JAMAICAN FEVERGRASS SAUCE

In Jamaica, 'fevergrass' is what we call lemongrass – it grows wild in certain parts of the island, but is not used in cooking. Instead, it is boiled down in water and used to make what we call a bush tea to bring down a fever. Here, we barbecue the lobsters and dress them with a simple chilli lime butter. A tart coconut, lime and fevergrass sauce is served on the side. The combination of flavours is out of this world!

Serves 4

1 tablespoon olive oil
2 tablespoons chopped garlic
1 teaspoon sea salt
freshly ground black pepper
3 tablespoons chopped fresh coriander
4 whole live lobsters, 450–675g each, split in half, or 4 x 225g lobster tails

For the Chilli Lime Butter

225g unsalted butter, at room temperature
1 bunch fresh coriander, finely chopped
juice of 6 limes (about 60ml)
grated zest of 1 lime
1 teaspoon chilli powder
pinch of sea salt

For the Fevergrass Culantro Sauce

(Makes about 250g)
180ml canned coconut milk (plus more if needed)
20g fresh coriander leaves
3 tablespoons chopped tender inner stalks lemongrass (from about 2 stalks)
2 spring onions, coarsely chopped
¼ teaspoon grated lime zest
1½ tablespoons fresh lime juice
¼ Scotch bonnet chilli, deseeded and very finely chopped
1 garlic clove, peeled
sea salt and freshly ground black pepper

Method

1 Place the oil, garlic, salt, a grind of pepper and coriander in a food processor and pulse to a paste. Rub the paste all over the insides of the lobsters and leave to stand in the refrigerator for at least 1 hour.

2 Meanwhile, to make the chilli lime butter, mix together all the ingredients in a small bowl. Set aside at room temperature.

3 To make the fevergrass culantro sauce, put the coconut milk, coriander, lemongrass, spring onions, lime zest and juice, Scotch bonnet and garlic in a blender and purée until smooth. Thin with more coconut milk by the teaspoonful, if desired. Season with salt and pepper. This can be made 1 day ahead and kept in the fridge.

4 Heat a gas or charcoal barbecue or a griddle pan over a high heat. Cook the lobsters cut side down; after 5 minutes, turn over and spread with the chilli lime butter. Cook for 5–8 minutes until firm. Serve with the fevergrass sauce on the side.

RACK OF LAMB WITH GRAPEFRUIT HONEY, AUBERGINE CAPONATA AND THREE-OLIVE RELISH

When we had to create meals for plated off-site dinners, we always liked to work with rack of lamb; it is easy to barbecue, holds well and is easy to plate. We created this dish for a sit-down family-style wedding by the seaside for a 150 people. The bride and groom were from London and really wanted lamb, so we came up with a Mediterranean presentation that could be served with some room-temperature sides, like this olive salsa and caponata. We catered the wedding as a hurricane was descending on the island, and every second we thought we would either be blown away or drowned in rain. We were lucky; we had a windy but dry evening, and the dish was very well received!

Serves 6

2 teaspoons very finely chopped garlic
¼ teaspoon very finely chopped Scotch bonnet chilli
1 tablespoon grated orange zest
2 tablespoons chopped fresh thyme
1 tablespoon chopped fresh rosemary
1 tablespoon chopped fresh mint
60ml extra virgin olive oil
sea salt and freshly ground black pepper
4 x 7-rib racks of lamb, trimmed

For the Three-Olive Relish

175g Kalamata olives, pitted and finely chopped
175g green olives, pitted and finely chopped
175g black olives, pitted and finely chopped
120ml olive oil
60ml orange juice
2 teaspoons grated orange zest
1 tablespoon honey, preferably Jamaican
1 teaspoon very finely chopped Scotch bonnet chilli
1 tablespoon chopped fresh thyme
1 tablespoon chopped fresh mint
2 tablespoons finely chopped roasted garlic
2 tablespoons very finely chopped red pepper
1 tablespoon very finely chopped red onion
sea salt and freshly ground black pepper

For the Aubergine Caponata

350ml vegetable oil
8 garlic cloves, peeled
pinch of dried mint
pinch of dried coriander
pinch of sea salt
3 medium aubergines, sliced
60ml olive oil

½ red onion, diced
25g spring onions, sliced
1 pepper, diced
80g raisins
60ml distilled white vinegar
2 tablespoons honey, preferably Jamaican
5 tablespoons chopped fresh coriander
2 tablespoons chopped fresh mint
sea salt and freshly ground black pepper

For the Honey Glaze

85g honey, preferably Jamaican
250ml grapefruit juice
1 tablespoon brown sugar
1 tablespoon chopped fresh thyme
2 tablespoons chopped fresh mint

Method

1 Put the garlic, Scotch bonnet, orange zest, thyme, rosemary, mint and oil in a medium bowl and whisk until blended, then season with salt and pepper. Place the lamb racks in a baking dish and pour the marinade over, working it into the meat with your hands. Refrigerate for a minimum of 3 hours.

2 To make the three-olive relish, put all the olives, the olive oil, orange juice and zest, honey, Scotch bonnet, thyme, mint, roasted garlic, red pepper and red onion in a medium bowl. Mix well and season with salt and pepper. Refrigerate for a minimum of 3 hours; the longer the relish sits, the better it tastes.

3 To make the aubergine caponata, preheat the oven to 200°C/gas mark 6. Put the vegetable oil, garlic, mint, coriander and salt in a large bowl. Add the aubergine slices and toss until well coated. Transfer the aubergine to a baking tray in a single layer and roast for 30 minutes until tender. Transfer to a chopping board, leave to cool and roughly chop. Transfer to a large bowl and set aside.

4 Warm the olive oil in a medium sauté pan. Add the red onion, spring onions, pepper and raisins and sauté for 3–5 minutes until softened. Add the vinegar and honey and cook down for 2–3 minutes. Stir in half the coriander and mint and transfer to the bowl with the aubergine. Season with salt and pepper, then add the rest of the coriander and mint to the bowl and toss well.

5 Allow the lamb to come to room temperature. Meanwhile, make the honey glaze. Combine the honey, grapefruit juice, brown sugar, thyme and mint in a small saucepan. Simmer over a medium heat for about 10 minutes until the glaze becomes syrupy.

6 Heat a gas or charcoal barbecue or a griddle pan over a medium heat. Sprinkle the lamb with a little salt just before putting it on the barbecue or in the pan to bring out the flavours. Cook for about 8 minutes until the outside is lightly marked, while basting with the honey glaze. If you wish, you can remove the racks of lamb before completely cooked through and finish them in a 180°C/gas mark 4 oven. The whole cooking process should not take more than 10 minutes per rack – you don't want to overcook the lamb.

7 Cut each rack into three or four cutlets of double ribs, place on serving plates, drizzle with the honey glaze and serve with dollops of the aubergine caponata and olive relish.

COCONUT PRAWNS FLAMBÉED IN RUM

This dish is a great option for last-minute entertaining, or a quick meal for one. We like to serve this over our Pumpkin Rice (page 142). We love to flambé with rum, a technique we usually do with desserts (like our Flambéed Bananas, page 166). When used in this savoury recipe, it brings out the subtle sweetness of the coconut cream, which is beautifully tempered with the spice of the Scotch bonnet and the tartness of the lime.

Serves 4

15g butter
4 spring onions, sliced
½ onion, chopped
3 garlic cloves, chopped
1 bunch fresh thyme, chopped
½ Scotch bonnet chilli, deseeded and very finely chopped
450g fresh or thawed frozen raw extra-large king or tiger prawns (10–16), peeled and deveined, tails left on
½ tablespoon sea salt
2 teaspoons freshly ground black pepper
60ml red rum
60ml canned coconut cream
1 lime, cut into wedges
fresh coriander leaves, for garnish

Method

1 Melt the butter in a frying pan over a medium heat. Add the spring onions, onion, garlic, thyme, Scotch bonnet and prawns and sauté for 5–8 minutes until opaque. Season with the salt and pepper, then add the rum and light it with a flame until the rum burns off. Add the coconut cream and cook for 3–5 minutes to reduce the liquid a bit.

2 Transfer the prawns and sauce to a plate, add a squeeze of lime and sprinkle with coriander.

MICHELLE'S CHARGRILLED BABY-BACK RIBS GLAZED WITH MOLASSES

These ribs are off da chain! The jerk and Scotch bonnet give them kick and the glaze adds a smoky sweetness. Feel free to leave out the spice; all we know is that once we start eating these, we can't stop! Serve with our Creole-Spiced Slaw (page 135) and Boiled Corn with Pimento Butter (page 140).

Serves 4–6

For the Molasses Glaze
3 tablespoons molasses
2 tablespoons tamari sauce
6 tablespoons hoisin sauce
60ml Thai sweet chilli sauce
60ml rum
6 allspice berries
2.5cm fresh ginger, peeled and sliced
2 tablespoons chopped fresh thyme
5 tablespoons honey
5 tablespoons brown sugar
240ml orange juice
60ml distilled white vinegar

1.8kg baby-back or pork ribs
1 bay leaf
7.5cm fresh ginger, peeled, plus
2 tablespoons peeled and grated
12 whole garlic cloves, peeled, plus 4 garlic
cloves, chopped
1 bunch fresh thyme
1 whole Scotch bonnet
1 bunch spring onions, plus 3, chopped
8 allspice berries
sea salt
1 tablespoon jerk sauce
3 tablespoons hoisin sauce
1 tablespoon honey
60ml Asian plum sauce
1 tablespoon soy sauce
2 tablespoons sesame or groundnut oil
2 tablespoons chopped fresh coriander

Method

1 To make the molasses glaze, put all the ingredients in a medium saucepan and bring to the boil, then reduce the heat to a simmer and cook for about 20 minutes until thickened.

2 Fill a saucepan big enough for the ribs with water. Add the bay leaf, 7.5cm ginger, garlic cloves, thyme, Scotch bonnet, whole spring onions and allspice and 1 teaspoon salt. Parboil the ribs for 25–30 minutes until the bones stick out at the edges. Transfer to a platter and leave to cool.

3 Mix together the jerk sauce, hoisin sauce, honey, plum sauce, soy sauce, sesame or groundnut oil, coriander, the 2 tablespoons grated ginger, the chopped garlic and a third of the chopped spring onions in a large stainless-steel bowl. Add the ribs and coat well with the marinade. Leave to stand in the fridge for at least 2 hours, but preferably overnight.

4 Bring the ribs back to room temperature before cooking. Heat a barbecue to a medium-high heat. Cook the ribs for 20–30 minutes, continually turning and basting with the glaze, until sticky and dark. Alternatively, preheat the oven to 200°C/gas mark 6, spread the ribs on a baking tray, drizzle with the glaze and roast for 30–40 minutes, basting with glaze.

5 Place the ribs on a platter and add the remaining chopped spring onions.

COOKING HINT

We've always boiled our ribs first because it saves time later when barbecuing fresh for a large event. However, you can skip this step and just marinate the ribs, bring to room temperature and barbecue them over a medium-low heat for about 1½ hours, turning them often. If you choose to roast them in the oven, it will also take about 1½ hours.

HERB-DUSTED MAHI-MAHI FILLET IN BANANA LEAVES WITH COCONUT LIME SALSA

Fresh mahi-mahi is marinated, topped with herb butter, wrapped in banana leaves and cooked on the barbecue. The banana leaves steam up delicious little parcels of fish that are bursting with flavour. Serve with a simple fresh coconut salsa and a light coconut sauce on the side. If fresh mahi-mahi is difficult to source, monkfish or swordfish make a good substitute.

Serves 4

1 teaspoon chopped fresh thyme
1 teaspoon sliced spring onion
1 teaspoon very finely chopped garlic
½ teaspoon sea salt
½ teaspoon freshly ground black pepper
2 teaspoons olive oil
1 tablespoon fresh lime juice, plus more for drizzling
900g mahi-mahi fillets, 175–225g each
banana leaves, cut into 25cm squares (or use foil squares)

For the Pimento Butter

115g unsalted butter
2 teaspoons ground allspice
3 spring onions, chopped
1 teaspoon chopped fresh thyme
1 garlic clove, peeled
juice of 2 limes
½ teaspoon sea salt

For the Coconut Lime Salsa

(MAKES ABOUT 240G)

130g grated fresh coconut or shredded unsweetened dried coconut
2 tablespoons fresh lime juice (from about 1½ limes)
3 tablespoons currants
2 tablespoons diced red onion
2 tablespoons chopped fresh coriander
½ teaspoon ground cumin
½ teaspoon sea salt
2 tablespoons olive oil

For the Coconut Sauce

(MAKES ABOUT 350ML)

1 x 400ml can coconut milk
1 tablespoon chopped fresh thyme
1 teaspoon very finely Scotch bonnet chilli
2 teaspoons diced spring onion
1 teaspoon diced onion
1 teaspoon very finely chopped garlic
sea salt and freshly ground black pepper

Method

1 Combine the thyme, spring onion, garlic, salt, pepper, oil and lime juice in a baking dish or resealable plastic bag. Add the mahi-mahi and leave to marinate in the fridge for about 2 hours.

2 To make the pimento butter, put the ingredients in a food processor and pulse until well combined.

3 To make the coconut lime salsa, mix together the coconut, lime juice, currants, red onion, coriander, cumin, salt and oil in a small bowl. Set aside.

4 To make the coconut sauce, combine the coconut milk with the thyme, Scotch bonnet, spring onion, onion and garlic in a medium saucepan over a medium heat and cook for about 5 minutes until slightly thickened. Season with salt and pepper.

5 Singe the banana leaves over an open flame, or blanch in a saucepan of boiling water and grease them with a little vegetable oil. Place one fish fillet inside each banana leaf square, dot with some pimento butter, add a squeeze of fresh lime and roll up each banana leaf to form a parcel (or use foil squares in the same way). Heat a gas or charcoal barbecue or a griddle pan over a medium heat (alternatively, preheat the oven to 180°C/gas mark 4), place the parcel seam side down and cook for 10–15 minutes until cooked through.

6 Cut open the parcels, place on serving plates and garnish with the coconut lime salsa. Serve the coconut sauce on the side.

GRILLED JERKED SALMON FILLET AND FRESH FRUIT SALSA

While the idea of jerk does not sound like it would work with salmon, it will surprise with how delicate the flavours are. The salmon is lightly marinated in pineapple juice, rum, pimento (allspice) and ginger, chargrilled to perfection, then served up on a bed of sweet potato purée and garnished with a mango papaya salsa. It is light, refreshing and a lovely change of pace for both the salmon and the jerk.

Serves 6

6 individual salmon fillets, about 225g each
1 lime, cut in half
60ml pineapple juice
60ml orange juice
6 tablespoons Appleton Special rum (or any dark rum)
1 tablespoon soy sauce
1 tablespoon chopped fresh thyme
2 tablespoons ground allspice
¼ teaspoon freshly grated nutmeg
½ teaspoon very finely chopped Scotch bonnet
1 teaspoon ground cinnamon
2 spring onions, very finely chopped
3 tablespoons finely chopped onion
sea salt and freshly ground black pepper
vegetable oil, for greasing

For the Tropical Fruit Salsa
(MAKES ABOUT 425G)
165g stoned and peeled mango, diced
145g peeled and deseeded papaya, diced
40g peeled and cored fresh pineapple, diced
1 teaspoon dried chilli flakes
juice of 2 limes
½ red pepper, diced
2 teaspoons finely diced spring onion
1 tablespoon chopped fresh coriander
sea salt and freshly ground pepper

Method

1 Rub the salmon fillets with the lime halves. Whisk together the pineapple juice, orange juice, rum, soy sauce, thyme, allspice, nutmeg, Scotch bonnet, cinnamon, spring onions, onion and salt and pepper in a large bowl. Add the salmon to the bowl and massage the marinade into the fillets. Cover with clingfilm and leave to stand in the fridge for at least 2 hours, turning the fillets every 30 minutes to ensure they are coated with the marinade.

2 Meanwhile, to make the tropical fruit salsa, put the mango, papaya, pineapple, chilli flakes, lime juice, red pepper, spring onion and coriander in a medium bowl and stir gently. Take care not to overmix the fruits because they will become soft and mushy. Season with salt and pepper. Refrigerate for 1 hour before serving.

3 Heat a gas or charcoal barbecue or a griddle pan to a medium heat and rub the barbecue rack or pan base with oil. Brush the marinade off the salmon and cook the fillets for 5–6 minutes per side, depending on the thickness, until your desired doneness. Turn the fillets only once so that they don't break apart during cooking.

4 Transfer the salmon to serving plates and spoon the fruit salsa alongside.

RED STRIPE BBQ PAN CHICKEN

This is our take on Jamaican Pan Chicken. The chicken is well marinated and basted repeatedly during barbecuing with our homemade Red Stripe BBQ sauce. It's spectacularly good! Feel free to use any beer you have available.

Serves 10

2.25kg chicken portions
60ml fresh lime juice or distilled white vinegar for washing
1 bunch spring onions, chopped
3 garlic cloves, very finely chopped
2.5cm fresh ginger, peeled and grated
½ Scotch bonnet chilli, finely chopped (optional)
2 tablespoons paprika
2 tablespoons olive oil
1 bunch fresh thyme, chopped
sea salt and freshly ground black pepper

For the Red Stripe BBQ Sauce

475g tomato ketchup
3 tablespoons tamari
3 tablespoons Pickapeppa sauce
70g brown sugar
3 tablespoons chopped spring onion
80ml distilled white vinegar
2 tablespoons peeled and grated fresh ginger
2 tablespoons Dijon mustard
2 tablespoons honey
3 garlic cloves, chopped
35g onion, chopped
1 Scotch bonnet chilli, deseeded and very finely chopped
180–240ml Red Stripe beer

Method

1 Wash the chicken in the lime or vinegar and rinse well under running water. Put the spring onions, garlic, ginger, Scotch bonnet, if using, paprika, oil, thyme and salt and pepper in a blender and blend to form a thick paste. Transfer to a baking dish or resealable plastic bag and add the chicken, tossing to coat. Season with more salt and pepper and leave to marinate in the fridge for 24 hours.

2 Preheat the oven to 180°C/gas mark 4.

3 To make the barbecue sauce, combine all the ingredients with just 120ml Red Stripe in a medium saucepan. Simmer for about 10 minutes, stirring occasionally, until thickened and reduced. Towards the end of the cooking time, add the rest of the Red Stripe (about 60–120ml). Divide the sauce between two bowls.

4 Heat a gas or charcoal barbecue to a medium-high heat. Dip the chicken in one bowl of the BBQ sauce and cook for about 30 minutes, continually turning the chicken and basting with the sauce throughout. Transfer the chicken pieces to a baking dish. Pour the BBQ sauce from the second bowl over the chicken pieces to coat them well.

5 Preheat the oven to 190°C/gas mark 5. Roast the chicken in the oven for 15–20 minutes until the sauce is nice and sticky and the chicken is cooked through, measuring 74°C on an instant-read thermometer.

6 Serve immediately.

BARBECUED CHICKEN WITH SPICY WEST INDIAN SALSA VERDE

This has to be our best-loved chicken dish. The well-seasoned chicken also gets a 'post-cooking' marinade; it is tossed in a bit of West Indian salsa verde and put in the oven for a few minutes so that the salsa verde flavours can be absorbed into the chicken. The combo of the chargrill, the island seasonings and the kick of the West Indian salsa verde is truly unforgettable.

Serves 8–10

60ml olive oil
1 bunch spring onions, sliced
8 garlic cloves, peeled
2 tablespoons peeled and grated fresh ginger
1 bunch fresh thyme
1 bunch fresh coriander
½ Scotch bonnet chilli, deseeded and very finely chopped
60ml fresh lime juice (from about 6 limes)
sea salt and freshly ground black pepper
1.8kg mixed chicken portions

For the Spicy West Indian Salsa Verde
(Makes about 700g)
50g fresh parsley, chopped
10g fresh chadon beni (culantro) or coriander, chopped
1 tablespoon roughly chopped garlic
50g spring onions, chopped
1 bunch fresh thyme, chopped
350ml olive oil
120ml water
6 tablespoons fresh lime juice (from about 8 limes)
2 teaspoons grated lime zest
1 Scotch bonnet chilli, cut in half and deseeded
1 tablespoon sea salt
1 tablespoon peeled and chopped fresh ginger

Method

1 Put the oil, spring onions, garlic, ginger, thyme, coriander, Scotch bonnet, lime juice and salt and pepper in a blender and blend to a purée. Transfer to a baking dish or resealable plastic bag and add the chicken, tossing to coat. Leave to marinate in the fridge for 12 hours or overnight.

2 Preheat the oven to 180°C/gas mark 4.

3 To make the spicy West Indian salsa verde, put the parsley, chadon beni or coriander, garlic, spring onions, thyme, oil, water, lime juice, lime zest, Scotch bonnet, salt and ginger in a food processor or blender and then blend well.

4 Heat a gas or charcoal barbecue or a griddle pan to a medium-high heat. Cook the chicken for about 10 minutes per side, turning once, until the outside is charred. Transfer the chicken to a baking dish and toss with the salsa verde, saving some for garnish. Bake for 10–15 minutes until the chicken is cooked through and an instant-read thermometer registers 74°C. Transfer the chicken to a platter, drizzle with more of the salsa verde and serve.

8

OUR ROOTS

GROUND PROVISIONS, SIDE DISHES AND VEGGIES

Sides and vegetables are rooted, yes, in the ground – but also in our history. Many Caribbean staples like yam, sweet potatoes, cassava, dasheen (taro), coco, plantain and green banana are inherited from our roots as a slave society. The mainstays of the slave diet were the starchy vegetables and ground provisions that provided energy and stamina for the long hours of back-breaking labour on a sugar plantation. Slaves were able to harvest many of these items for themselves. This reliance on root vegetables, along with one-pot dishes and the introduction of rice, has shaped many of the traditional meals that we still eat in the Caribbean today.

The modern Caribbean diet continues to incorporate many of these starchy vegetables as accompaniments to small amounts of protein in our daily meals. We love ground provisions, not only because of their superior nutritional value, but also for the diversity of their flavours and textures, which allows for variety at the dinner table and inspires great creativity. In this chapter, we share longtime favourites along with new, innovative side dishes with Caribbean flair.

SWEET POTATO GRATIN

There is nothing that can adequately express how yummy this dish is! This is our kind of comfort food – just give it a try. We like to serve it with Mummy's roast pork (page 82) or our jerked pork (page 100). Also it's a perfect side dish for Christmas dinner.

Serves 6-8

900g sweet potatoes, peeled and cut into cubes
700ml double cream
25g spring onions, chopped
½ onion, chopped
½ teaspoon chopped fresh thyme
½ Scotch bonnet chilli, deseeded and very finely chopped
4 garlic cloves, finely chopped
sea salt and freshly ground black pepper
100g Parmesan cheese, freshly grated
45g panko (Japanese) breadcrumbs

Method

1 Preheat the oven to 180°C/gas mark 4.

2 Bring a large saucepan of salted water to the boil over a high heat. Add the sweet potatoes and boil for 20–25 minutes until cooked through.

3 Meanwhile, put the cream, spring onions, onion, thyme, Scotch bonnet and garlic in a small saucepan, bring to the boil and then leave to simmer for 10 minutes.

4 When the sweet potatoes are soft, drain and transfer to a large mixing bowl, then mash until smooth. Pour in the cream mixture, season to taste with salt and pepper and stir in half the Parmesan. Transfer to a baking dish and top with the remaining Parmesan and the breadcrumbs. Bake for 35 minutes or until the cheese and breadcrumbs are golden brown. Serve immediately.

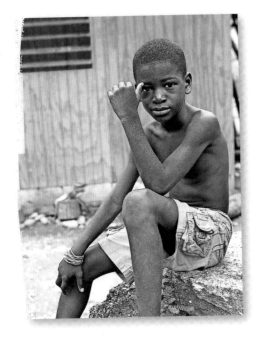

SMASHED YAM

In Jamaica, a yam is very different from what they call 'yams' in the USA; our yams are more dense and hearty. The yam was originally imported from Africa, and this starchy, nutrient-rich vegetable became the preferred food of slaves working the Caribbean plantations. It is also the food of champions: when Jamaican gold medalist Usain Bolt was asked what the source of his speed was, after breaking his first world record for the 100- and 200-metre sprints, he replied that it's all in the yams. Traditionally, yam was roasted over an open flame or boiled in salted water. Here, we use the yam to make a supremely satisfying casserole.

Serves 10-12

1.1kg yellow yam, peeled and cubed (see page 23)
30g butter
1 tablespoon very finely chopped onion
1 teaspoon very finely chopped garlic
1 spring onion, very finely chopped
2 teaspoons chopped fresh thyme
2 teaspoons plain flour
240ml milk
240ml double cream
60ml white wine
sea salt and freshly ground pepper
60g Cheddar cheese, grated
50g Parmesan cheese, freshly grated

Method

1 Preheat the oven to 180°C/gas mark 4. Butter a baking dish.

2 Bring a large saucepan of salted water to the boil over a medium-high heat. Add the yam and boil for 25–30 minutes until soft. Drain.

3 Meanwhile, melt the butter in a saucepan over a medium heat. Add the onion, garlic, spring onion and thyme and cook until the vegetables are wilted. Stir in the flour and cook for about 2 minutes until the flour is no longer raw. Gradually pour in the milk and cream in small amounts, whisking continually, until the sauce thickens. Add the white wine, season with salt and pepper and remove the sauce from the heat.

4 Transfer the cooked yam to a large bowl and mash with a fork, leaving it quite lumpy. Add the cream sauce along with half the Cheddar and mix well. Season with salt and pepper. Place in the prepared baking dish and then sprinkle with the rest of the Cheddar and the Parmesan. Bake for 35 minutes until nice and bubbly. Serve immediately.

INGREDIENT NOTE

Many varieties of this root vegetable are available in Jamaica — yellow yam, yampee, white yam — and they are all delicious and incredibly nutritious. Try shopping at a Caribbean food shop or market and asking for one of these varieties, or you can substitute dasheen (taro) root.

SWEET POTATO PURÉE WITH TOASTED PECANS AND BROWN SUGAR

Here is another tasty recipe for this popular starch, which mixes citric tastes with a creamy purée and tops it off with brown sugar and toasted pecans. It is a great side dish for the holiday season.

Serves 10-12

2.25kg sweet potatoes, peeled and cut into cubes
30g butter
475ml double cream
1 tablespoon grated orange zest
120ml orange juice
4 tablespoons brown sugar
1 teaspoon ground cinnamon
sea salt and freshly ground black pepper
50g raw pecan nuts, toasted

Method

1 Preheat the oven to 180°C/gas mark 4.

2 Bring a large saucepan of salted water to the boil. Add the sweet potatoes to the pan and cook for 20–30 minutes until soft. Drain, transfer to a blender and purée, or mash by hand.

3 Meanwhile, melt the butter in a small saucepan over a medium heat. Add the cream and orange zest and juice. Whisk in about 1 tablespoon of the brown sugar and the cinnamon and simmer for about 8 minutes until thickened.

4 Pour the cream sauce over the mashed sweet potatoes and mix to combine. Season with salt and pepper and spread in a baking dish. Sprinkle with the remaining 3 tablespoons brown sugar and the pecans and bake for 35–40 minutes until the top is crusty. Serve immediately.

RUM BROWN SUGAR PLANTAINS

Plantain is served as a side dish at almost every meal in the islands. In Jamaica, we eat it both ripe and green, but most often it is sliced ripe and fried in a little vegetable oil. Here, we slow bake it in guava, brown sugar and cinnamon until caramelised and golden. It's great with curries or any kind of meat.

Serves 6-8

60ml dark rum
55g brown sugar
350ml guava juice (or any available fruit juice)
1 teaspoon ground cinnamon
¼ teaspoon freshly grated nutmeg
½ teaspoon ground allspice
3 tablespoons honey
6 large ripe plantains, peeled
45g butter, cut into small pieces
orange zest, for garnish

Method

1 Preheat the oven to 200°C/gas mark 6.

2 Whisk together the rum, sugar, guava juice, cinnamon, nutmeg, allspice and honey in a medium bowl. Place the plantains in a small roasting tin, pour the sauce over the top and dot the tops with the butter. Roast the plantains for about 40 minutes, turning and basting them frequently. Reduce the heat to 160°C/gas mark 3 and roast for another 35 minutes or until the sauce is reduced and syrupy and the plantains are soft.

3 Transfer the plantains to a platter and slice on the bias. Pour any sauce remaining in the pan over the top, garnish with orange zest and serve.

ROASTED MIXED POTATOES

Simple, easy and satisfying, this dish is the perfect complement to any roast. These potatoes rock with our Marmalade-Glazed Leg of Lamb (page 86)!

Serves 8

900g sweet potatoes, peeled and cut into cubes
900g baking potatoes, peeled and cut into cubes
60ml olive oil
sea salt and freshly ground black pepper
4 garlic cloves, sliced
2 tablespoons fresh rosemary leaves
2 tablespoons fresh thyme leaves

Method

1 Preheat the oven to 200°C/gas mark 6.

2 Toss the potatoes with the oil, salt and pepper, garlic, rosemary and thyme in a large bowl. Leave to stand for 15 minutes to allow the flavours to develop.

3 Spread out the potatoes in a thin layer on a baking sheet and roast for 15 minutes, until brown and crispy. Lower the heat to 180°C/gas mark 4 and roast until cooked through. Serve hot.

TRINI CORN PIE

One of the Trinidadian dishes we love most is corn pie. At large family meals, almost every home will have this side dish, which is more like a pudding, made with both sweetcorn kernels and creamed corn.

Serves 6

85g canned sweetcorn kernels, drained and liquid reserved
1 medium egg, at room temperature
½ teaspoon sea salt
½ teaspoon freshly ground white pepper
8 tablespoons finely ground cornmeal
55g salted butter, plus more for greasing
100g onions, chopped
115g pepper, chopped
½ Scotch bonnet chilli, deseeded and very finely chopped, or to taste
475g canned evaporated milk
2 tablespoons chopped fresh coriander
130g creamed-style corn
115g mature Cheddar cheese, grated

Method

1 Preheat the oven to 180°C/gas mark 4. Grease a baking dish with butter.

2 Pour the reserved sweetcorn liquid into a measuring jug. Top up with enough lukewarm water to make 240ml. Pour the liquid and egg into a large bowl. Add the salt and white pepper and beat to mix well. Add the cornmeal and stir to form a smooth paste. Set aside.

3 Melt the butter in a medium saucepan over a medium heat. Add the onions, peppers and Scotch bonnet and sauté until the onions are translucent. Pour in the evaporated milk and bring the mixture to the boil. Immediately stir in the cornmeal paste and reduce the heat to low; cook for 4 minutes, stirring intermittently.

4 Stir in the sweetcorn kernels. Cook over a low heat for about 5 minutes until the mixture comes away easily from the sides of the pan.

5 Remove the pan from the heat and stir in the coriander, creamed corn and half the cheese. Transfer to the prepared baking dish, smooth the surface and sprinkle the remaining cheese on top. Bake for 30 minutes or until the cheese is melted and golden brown.

6 Leave to rest for at least 30 minutes before cutting and serving.

TWICE-ROASTED LOCAL MIXED VEGETABLES

This vegetable dish is bursting with so many wonderful flavours and textures that it will blow your mind! Your friends and family are sure to keep coming back for more. We like to serve this alongside the Barbecued Chicken with Spicy West Indian Salsa Verde (page 122).

Serves 4–6

5 plum tomatoes, quartered
4–5 garlic cloves, peeled
2 onions, quartered
2 tablespoons olive oil, plus 60ml
1 bunch fresh rosemary, chopped
1 bunch fresh thyme, chopped
sea salt and freshly ground black pepper
1½ ripe plantains, cut into cubes
3 carrots, peeled and cut into cubes
2 red and yellow peppers, cut into cubes
2 cho cho (chayote), peeled and cut into cubes (see page 23)
110g trimmed green beans
200g cauliflower florets
230g peeled and deseeded calabaza pumpkin or other starchy squash, such as butternut, cubed

Method

1 Preheat the oven to 200°C/gas mark 6.

2 Toss the tomatoes, garlic cloves and onions with the 2 tablespoons oil and half the rosemary and thyme in a large baking dish. Season with salt and pepper and roast for 20 minutes until all the vegetables are soft and the tomatoes have released their juices. Remove from the oven and toss well so that tomato juice coats all the vegetables.

3 Mix together the plantains, carrots, red and yellow peppers, cho cho, beans, cauliflower and pumpkin in a large bowl. Season with a generous quantity of salt, the remaining herbs and the remaining 60ml oil. Add the uncooked vegetable mixture to the tomato, onion and garlic mixture and toss to combine. Roast for another 20–25 minutes until all the vegetables are cooked through but still firm. Serve hot.

CHO CHO PACKETS

Inspired by a delicious recipe from Jamie Oliver, we decided to try cho cho a new way and roast-steam them in these delightful packets of flavour. These would be a great accompaniment to our whole roast snapper (page 107) or barbecued jerked salmon (page 120).

Serves 6–8

6 cho cho (chayote), peeled and sliced (see page 23)
120ml white wine
1 bunch fresh thyme
sea salt and freshly ground black pepper
70g salted butter, cut into pieces

Method

1 Preheat the oven to 180°C/gas mark 4.

2 Place a large square of foil on a baking tray and fold up the sides. Add the cho cho and pour the white wine over the top. Add the thyme and season with salt and pepper. Dot with the butter and close up the foil to make a packet. Roast for 35 minutes until the cho cho is tender.

3 Cut open the foil packet and serve hot.

CREOLE-SPICED SLAW

We made this dish for a fabulous island-themed rehearsal dinner that we catered in the Hamptons for our great friend, television personality Robyn Moreno. None of the guests was from the Caribbean, although we did have a few Tejanos and they simply loved the island flava! This cool summer slaw is spicy-sweet perfection with any kind of barbecue – from burgers to ribs to chicken. Enjoy!

Serves 6

For the Sweet and Spicy Jerked Cashews
170g raw cashew nuts
2 teaspoons jerk sauce
sea salt
15g butter
3 tablespoons brown sugar

For the Coconut Sesame Dressing
juice of 6 limes (about 6 tablespoons)
1 stalk lemongrass, tender inner part only, smashed and finely chopped
1 spring onion, chopped
2 tablespoons honey, preferably Jamaican
1 tablespoon brown sugar
2 tablespoons toasted sesame oil
1 teaspoon soy sauce
¼ teaspoon very finely chopped Scotch bonnet
60ml canned coconut milk
sea salt and freshly ground black pepper

175g white cabbage, thinly shredded
175g red cabbage, thinly shredded
½ medium red pepper, cut into matchsticks
½ medium yellow pepper, cut into matchsticks
1 red chilli, deseeded and finely sliced into strips
½ red onion, thinly sliced
85g peeled and cored fresh pineapple, cut into thinly sliced strips
1 ripe mango, stoned, peeled and cut into thin strips
1 medium ripe papaya, peeled, deseeded and cut into thin strips
sea salt and freshly ground black pepper
1 bunch fresh mint, chopped
1 bunch fresh coriander, chopped
toasted grated fresh coconut or shredded unsweetened dried coconut (optional)

Method

1 To make the sweet and spicy jerked cashews, preheat the oven to 180°C/gas mark 4. Toss the cashews with the jerk sauce and a little salt in a small bowl. Spread out on a baking tray in a single layer and toast in the oven for about 5 minutes until golden.

2 Melt the butter in a saucepan over a medium heat. Add the brown sugar and leave to melt. When the sugar begins to caramelise, add the roasted cashews and toss to coat well. Spread the cashews out on a baking tray lined with greaseproof paper to cool. Roughly chop.

3 To make the coconut sesame dressing, put all the ingredients in a blender and whizz together. Season with salt and pepper.

4 Mix together both cabbages, the peppers, chilli, red onion, pineapple, mango and papaya in a large bowl. Season with salt and pepper. Pour the dressing over the vegetable and fruit mixture, add the mint and coriander and toss. Top with the sweet and spicy cashews and toasted coconut, if using. Serve chilled.

ROASTED PUMPKIN AND FIGS WITH LIME TAHINI

Michelle was obsessed with this dish when she lived in Fort Greene, Brooklyn, and had access to the farmers' market. When figs came into season, it was all she wanted – the bright mint paired with the tang of the lime tahini, the sweetness of the pumpkin and figs and the crisp of the roasted garlic! Add spice to the tahini by throwing in some slivered Thai green chillies. It makes a great dipping sauce, too.

Serves 6

1.8kg pumpkin, peeled and chopped
8 fresh figs, quartered
½ red onion, sliced
8 garlic cloves, peeled
60ml olive oil
1 bunch fresh mint, chopped
sea salt and freshly ground black pepper
Chadon Beni Oil (page 46)

For the Lime Tahini

juice of 2 limes
1 teaspoon honey
60ml hot water, plus more if needed
60ml tahini
1 teaspoon peeled and grated fresh ginger
2 tablespoons chopped fresh mint
1 tablespoon chopped fresh coriander

Method

1 Preheat the oven to 200°C/gas mark 6. On a large baking tray, toss the pumpkin, figs, red onion and garlic cloves with the oil. Sprinkle with the mint and season well with salt and pepper. Roast for about 20 minutes or until caramelised.

2 Meanwhile, to make the lime tahini, in a small bowl, whisk together the lime juice, honey, hot water and tahini. Add the ginger, mint and coriander. Season with salt and pepper and thin with a little more water or some olive oil as needed.

3 Assemble the roasted vegetables on a platter. Drizzle with the tahini sauce and chadon beni oil just before serving.

GREEN BEANS WITH GINGER AND GARLIC

Green beans are one of the few vegetables that you can always get at the local market here, and we always try to stay local. Finding delicious and creative ways to prepare them has always been a challenge. This dish is extremely simple, but very tasty and goes with just about any kind of protein!

Serves 6–8

675–900g green beans, trimmed
15g salted butter
1 tablespoon olive oil
4 garlic cloves, very finely chopped
2.5cm fresh ginger, peeled and very finely chopped
1 bunch fresh thyme, chopped
1 bunch fresh mint, chopped
sea salt and freshly ground black pepper

Method

1 Blanch the green beans in a large saucepan of salted boiling water for about 5 minutes until bright green. Transfer to a colander and immediately run under cold water to stop the cooking process. Don't overcook the beans; they should be bright and fresh in colour with a crunch.

2 Melt the butter and oil in a sauté pan over a medium heat. Add the garlic and ginger and cook until golden brown and crispy, but be careful not to let them burn! Add the thyme and mint, then quickly toss in the beans. Season with salt and pepper and serve.

INGREDIENT NOTE

Feel free to use ripe plantains
or sweet potatoes, which are
not as dense as pumpkin but work
really well, too. Any other kind of
squash or starchy vegetable can also
be substituted.

TWICE-FRIED PRESSED GREEN PLANTAIN WITH AVOCADO, CORIANDER AND MANCHEGO

This easy snack is an unexpectedly delectable treat. As simple as it looks, you will be utterly but pleasantly surprised by the burst of flavours that awaken your taste buds as you bite into the hot plantain. Your guests will not be able to stop talking about it – if there's actually any left for them, that is.

Serves 8

2 large green plantains
about 700ml vegetable or coconut oil
sea salt and freshly ground black pepper
1 large avocado, stoned, peeled and sliced
1 bunch spring onions, chopped
2 tablespoons fresh lime juice, or to taste
115g Manchego cheese, grated
1 bunch chopped fresh coriander
65g Spicy West Indian Salsa Verde (page 122)

Method

1 Cut off both ends of each plantain and, with the tip of a paring knife, score lengthways along the ridges of the plantain skin; peel away the skin. Cut the plantains into 5cm-thick pieces and sprinkle with salt.

2 Heat about 10cm oil in a large saucepan over a high heat. Once the oil is very hot, drop the plantain pieces into the oil and fry for about 2 minutes. Transfer the plantains to a plate lined with kitchen paper to drain. Reserve the oil in the pan.

3 Spread a clean tea towel on a work surface, place one piece of fried plantain on the cloth and fold the cloth over the plantain; press hard with the heel of your hand to flatten the plantain to about 1cm thick. Repeat with the remaining pieces of plantain. Once all the plantains are pressed, heat the oil up again and fry the plantains for a further 3 minutes or until golden brown. Transfer to a plate lined with fresh kitchen paper to drain. Season with salt.

4 Mash the avocado with the spring onions, a pinch of salt and the lime juice in a small bowl.

5 Place some mashed avocado on top of each pressed plantain and top with the cheese, coriander and a generous drizzle of spicy salsa verde. Serve immediately.

MAMA'S BANANA FRITTERS

Our grandmother, Mama, made these with her leftover overripe bananas at the end of the week and served them with her meatloaf and rice and peas. We'd steal them from the kitchen and munch away without her ever knowing we were there – we're smooth like that! Serve as a side dish or tasty snack.

Serves 10

6 overripe bananas
2 teaspoons vanilla extract
¼ teaspoon freshly grated nutmeg
125g plain flour
120ml full-fat milk or water
3 tablespoons vegetable oil
½ teaspoon ground cinnamon
2 tablespoons sugar

Method

1 Mash the bananas in a large bowl with a fork until they form a smooth, wet purée. Mix in the vanilla and nutmeg. Add the flour and the milk or water and mix to thoroughly combine.

2 Heat the oil in a large frying pan over a medium heat. Drop tablespoonfuls of the banana mixture into the oil and fry until golden on one side. Flip over and fry for another 2 minutes. Transfer to kitchen paper to drain.

3 Mix the cinnamon and sugar together and sprinkle over the hot fritters.

GREEN BANANAS STEWED IN COCONUT MILK

We ate this dish for the first time when we were teenagers, at the country home of a well-known Jamaican artist, Judy Ann Macmillan, in St Ann – and we have never forgotten it. The green bananas were stewed in a Dutch oven over an outdoor fire and served with an array of barbecued meats. It was one of the simplest and most memorable meals we have ever had – authentic Jamaican country cooking.

Serves 4

2 spring onions, finely chopped
¼ onion, finely chopped
¼ Scotch bonnet chilli, deseeded and finely chopped
1 bunch fresh thyme, finely chopped
475ml canned coconut milk
475ml water
1 bay leaf
1 teaspoon sea salt
12 medium green bananas, peeled and quartered (see page 148)
freshly ground black pepper

Method

1 Mix together the spring onions, onion, Scotch bonnet and thyme in a small bowl.

2 Bring the coconut milk, water, bay leaf, thyme and salt to the boil in a large saucepan. Add the onion mixture and bananas to the pan and return to the boil. Reduce the heat and simmer for about 1 hour until the coconut milk forms a custard.

3 Divide between four bowls, grind some fresh black pepper over the top and serve.

BOILED CORN WITH PIMENTO BUTTER AND CHEESE

When Michelle lived in Fort Greene, Brooklyn, every Saturday she would head to the Fort Greene Flea Market to browse, chill a bit, buy a doughnut (or six) from Dough and eat corn on the cob rolled in chilli and sprinkled with Mexican cheese. This is our ode to that dish, but we've added a little 'Yardie', or Jamaican, flavour.

Serves 6

2.8 litres water
450g butter
1 bunch spring onions
4 garlic cloves, peeled
6 Scotch bonnet chillies
2 tablespoons sea salt
1 bunch fresh thyme
6 allspice berries
2 bay leaves
6 corn on the cob, husks reserved
115g Pimento Butter (page 119)
115g Asiago cheese, grated
Spiced Salt (page 55), to taste
3 fresh limes
3 tablespoons chopped fresh coriander

Method

1 Put the water, butter, spring onions, garlic cloves, Scotch bonnets, salt, thyme, allspice and bay leaves in a large saucepan and bring to the boil. Add the corn cobs and boil for about 20 minutes until the corn is very tender.

2 With tongs, remove the corn cobs from the water. Roll each corn cob first in the pimento butter, then in the cheese, then return the cobs to their husks. Garnish each corn cob with some spiced salt, a squeeze of fresh lime juice and the coriander. Serve immediately.

COCONUT JASMINE FRIED RICE PILAF WITH CASHEWS AND RAISINS

The sweetness of the raisins combined with the crunch of the cashews add complexity to the flavour and texture of this rice pilaf. This is outstanding with garlic or coconut prawns (pages 104 or 115).

Serves 10

475ml water
1 x 400ml can coconut milk
2 teaspoons sea salt, plus more for seasoning
450g fragrant jasmine rice
2 tablespoons coconut oil
½ onion, chopped
2 tablespoons chopped garlic
1 teaspoon peeled and grated ginger
2 spring onions, chopped
2 tablespoons chopped fresh thyme
grated zest of ½ lime
1 teaspoon very finely chopped Scotch bonnet
85g raisins
135g raw cashew nuts, toasted
freshly ground black pepper
2 tablespoons chopped fresh coriander

Method

1 Put the water, coconut milk and salt in a large saucepan and bring to the boil. Add the rice, reduce the heat to low and cook, covered, for 25 minutes.

2 Heat half the oil in a sauté pan and add half the onion, garlic, ginger, spring onions, thyme, lime zest, Scotch bonnet, raisins and cashews. Sauté for 3–5 minutes over a medium heat until the onions are translucent. Season with salt and pepper. Add half the rice and toss together. Transfer to a large bowl and repeat with the remaining ingredients.

3 Sprinkle the coriander on top and serve.

RICE AND PEAS (OR GUNGO PEAS)

All islands have some version of rice and peas, and every island chef has his own recipe or way of making it; here's ours! We always use dried peas when making this except during Christmastime when fresh gungo, or pigeon, peas are available (see the Cooking Hint opposite).

Serves 12

400g dried red cow peas or dried gungo (pigeon) peas (but see Cooking Hint opposite)
1.1 litres cold water
3 garlic cloves, peeled
1 x 400ml can coconut milk
2.5cm fresh ginger, peeled and grated
3–4 spring onions, chopped
1 bunch fresh thyme, chopped
1 whole Scotch bonnet chilli
6 allspice berries
1 tablespoon sea salt
freshly ground black pepper
675g white long-grain rice

Method

1 Add the peas to the cold water in a large bowl and soak overnight.

2 Transfer the peas and soaking water to a large saucepan, add the garlic and bring to the boil. Reduce the heat and simmer for 40 minutes or until the peas are cooked. Add the coconut milk, ginger, spring onions, thyme, Scotch bonnet, allspice, salt and a few grinds of pepper. Simmer for 20 minutes, reduce the heat to low, add the rice and stir once. Cover and cook for a further 30 minutes until all the water is absorbed. Remove the whole Scotch bonnet and serve.

Variation: For a quick rice and peas using canned beans, bring 475ml cold water to the boil with all the seasonings, coconut milk and drained canned peas. Stir in the rice and bring to the boil, reduce the heat, cover and simmer for 30 minutes until the liquid is evaporated.

PUMPKIN RICE

We love pumpkin rice – when the flavours in the dish meld together, it is a magical experience. It makes a great side dish, but is also good enough to be eaten as a meal on its own!

Serves 12

450g calabaza pumpkin or other starchy squash, such as butternut, peeled and deseeded
1 tablespoon olive oil
1 spring onion, chopped
½ onion, chopped
3 garlic cloves, chopped
1 bunch fresh thyme, chopped
1 teaspoon sea salt
½ teaspoon freshly ground black pepper
700ml hot water
1 x 400ml can coconut milk
2 bay leaves
1 whole Scotch bonnet
450g rice, preferably basmati or fragrant jasmine
30g butter

Method

1 Chop half the pumpkin into a fine dice, and roughly chop the other half.

2 Warm the oil in a sauté pan over a medium heat. Add the spring onion, onion and garlic and cook for 2–3 minutes. Add the pumpkin, thyme, salt and pepper and sauté for about 5 minutes. Add the hot water, coconut milk, bay leaves and Scotch bonnet and bring to the boil. Gently stir in the rice and return to the boil. Add the butter, reduce the heat to low, cover and simmer for 30 minutes until the rice is cooked and all the liquid has been absorbed. Carefully remove the whole Scotch bonnet and serve.

COOKING HINT

If you are using fresh gungo peas, simmer them in 700ml water with all the seasonings and the coconut milk for about 20 minutes. Add the rice, cover and simmer for another 30 minutes until cooked. Total cooking time is 50 minutes.

9

RISE AND SHINE

BREAKFAST AND BRUNCH

Every morning when we were kids, with annoying regularity, our father would wake us up for school by turning on the lights and shouting at the top of his lungs: 'Rise and shine, rise and shine!' But now we know, he just wanted to make sure we had time to eat a healthy breakfast before school. Breakfast is important family time; memories of morning meals spent with our grandparents and at home still linger.

Michelle was a porridge baby; Suzanne hated eggs. Here, we share recipes re-created from our fondest breakfast memories – morning meals from Norbrook Road in Kingston to Nutmeg Avenue in Port of Spain and everywhere else in between. These flavours from our childhood still influence our breakfast favourites to this day, and often show up on event menus and on our breakfast tables at home.

CAFÉ BELLA'S BRIOCHE FRENCH TOAST

The best French toast is made with brioche bread; its slightly sweet flavour and light texture make it fluffy, yummy and très chic. We like to top our French toast with bananas and Nutella, but feel free to substitute your fruit of choice and the more standard maple syrup instead. This was a favourite brunch item at our restaurant, Café Bella.

Serves 4

2 tablespoons coconut milk
60ml milk
1 medium egg
2 teaspoons vanilla extract
dash of freshly grated nutmeg
60g butter
4 thick slices brioche bread
1 large banana, sliced
4 teaspoons Nutella (or other hazelnut-chocolate spread)
1 tablespoon icing sugar

Method

1 Put the coconut milk, milk, egg, vanilla and nutmeg in a medium bowl and whisk until well combined.

2 Melt 15g of the butter in a frying pan over a medium heat. One piece at a time, soak the bread in the milk mixture and cook for about 2 minutes on each side until browned on both sides. Transfer to a plate and keep warm. Add another 15g butter to the pan and repeat with another piece of bread until all four slices are browned.

3 Top each slice of French toast with sliced bananas, 1 teaspoon Nutella and a dusting of icing sugar.

NUTTY GRANOLA

One of our favourite ways to start the day is with creamy yogurt, homemade granola and the crunch of nuts, the sweetness of fresh fruit and a drizzle of honey. If you love granola as much as we do, try this version, which is cooked low and slow for 1½ hours.

Serves 12

325g rolled oats
70g roasted almonds
70g sea salted cashew nuts
70g shelled pistachio nuts
85g grated fresh coconut or shredded unsweetened dried coconut
55g brown sugar
2 tablespoons honey
60ml olive oil
1 teaspoon sea salt
165g raisins
95g dried apricots, sliced

Method

1 Preheat the oven to 120°C/gas mark ½.

2 Mix together the oats, almonds, cashews, pistachios, coconut and brown sugar in a large bowl. In another bowl, mix together the honey, oil and salt. Pour the wet mixture onto the dry mixture and stir to coat, then spread out on two baking trays.

3 Bake for 1½ hours, turning the granola with a spatula every 15 minutes or so to ensure an even toasty colour. Transfer to a large bowl, then mix in the raisins and apricots. Store in an airtight container for up to 2 weeks.

GENIE'S CORNMEAL PORRIDGE WITH COCONUT AND BAY LEAF

Traditionally in Jamaica, porridge is breakfast food – a tradition most likely inherited from the wave of Scottish migrants that came to Jamaica in the early 1900s. Our great grandfather, McAllister, was one among them. Porridge is often the go-to food for 'pickney' (Jamaican speak for kids or children) and babies. Country folks say that porridge babies are strong, healthy and 'traptin' (strapping)! We particularly love this version, which Imogene Brown (aka Genie) used to make for us and our catering team for breakfast on those eternally long workdays that started before dawn. We added a couple bay leaves for a subtly different flavour that is simply delicious.

Serves 6

950ml water, plus more for thinning
700ml freshly made coconut milk
(see page 24) or 1 x 400ml can coconut milk mixed with 300ml water
2 bay leaves
185g fine cornmeal
¼ teaspoon sea salt
2 teaspoons vanilla extract
½ whole nutmeg, freshly grated
105g brown sugar
180ml sweetened condensed milk, or to taste (optional)

Method

1 Put 700ml of the water, the coconut milk and bay leaves in a large saucepan and bring to the boil.

2 Meanwhile, mix the cornmeal with the remaining 250ml water so that the cornmeal does not become lumpy when added to the coconut milk mixture. Once the coconut milk is boiling, add the salt, then pour in the cornmeal mixture and start whisking right away. Reduce the heat to medium-low and continue whisking so that the cornmeal does not get lumpy. Reduce the heat to low and simmer for a further 20 minutes, whisking every 2 minutes or so. If the porridge gets too thick, add more water as needed.

3 When ready to serve, remove the bay leaves and add the vanilla, nutmeg, brown sugar and, if desired, condensed milk to taste.

COOKING TIP

The key to making a good Jamaican porridge is the inclusion of both nutmeg and vanilla. It's also very important not to have a lumpy porridge, so stir well and consistently to avoid any lumps!

HYACINTH'S GREEN BANANA PORRIDGE

In Jamaica, we love porridge so much that we turn everything we can into porridge – cornmeal, hominy corn, peanut, cashew, green plantain, oats, you name it! We particularly love Hyacinth's green banana porridge; the addition of oats makes for a hearty and healthy meal. This is island-style comfort food at its best. It makes a great (albeit different) supper on a cold winter's night!

Serves 8

6 medium-green small bananas, peeled (see Cooking Note)
2 tablespoons plain flour
2 tablespoons oats
240ml milk
950ml water
50g coconut milk powder mixed with 2 tablespoons water
2 teaspoons vanilla extract
dash of freshly grated nutmeg
dash of ground cinnamon
pinch of sea salt
2 tablespoons brown sugar, or to taste
2 tablespoons sweetened condensed milk, or to taste (optional)

Method

1 Grate the bananas on a hand-held grater into a bowl (or you could finely chop them in a food processor). Mix in the flour, oats and milk.

2 In the meantime, bring the water to the boil in a heavy-based saucepan. Add the banana mixture and, stirring constantly so that it doesn't get lumpy, return the mixture to the boil.

3 Reduce the heat to medium or low and simmer for about 10 minutes, continuing to stir so that the porridge doesn't develop lumps. Once it has thickened a bit and the mixture has begun to cook (you will see it come together), stir in the coconut milk, vanilla, nutmeg, cinnamon and salt. Bring to the boil while stirring, then turn the heat all the way down to low, cover and simmer without stirring for 35–40 minutes.

4 Remove from the heat and mix in the brown sugar and condensed milk, if using; taste and adjust the seasoning, adding more vanilla, coconut milk, cow's milk or nutmeg as desired. The porridge should be thick and smooth. Serve piping hot!

COOKING NOTE

Before peeling the green bananas, rub 1 teaspoon vegetable oil on your hands (or alternatively, you could peel the bananas under running water); the bananas are very starchy and your hands will become sticky. Place a bowl of water near your chopping board; you'll add the peeled bananas to the water so that they don't turn brown. Cut off the stem end of a banana. Score a deep cut down the side of the banana with the tip of the knife, then cut off the other end of the banana. Peel off the skin using your hands and use the edge of the knife to scrape away any excess strings of skin. Place in the bowl of water until ready to cook. Repeat with the other bananas.

TRINI-STYLE SALT FISH AND BAKE

All of our islands cook salt fish (salt cod) in one way or another for breakfast, lunch and even dinner. As our childhood years were spent in Trinidad, we favour this Trini version, known there as buljol. Salt fish is often served alongside some kind of fried dumpling, some fluffy and large, others smaller and dense. In Jamaica, we serve salt fish with johnnycakes – small, round fried dumplings. Other countries, like Trinidad and Guyana, call them 'bake', and they are usually the size of a small pitta bread. Here, we pair this traditional Trini salt fish with our version of a bake – a hybrid recipe inspired by the bakes served in Trinidad, Guyana and Belize. If you have any left over, these little breads are also great topped with Cheddar cheese and guava jam, or even just butter and jam.

Serves 6–8

For the Trini-Style Salt Fish
250g boiled, picked and cleaned salt fish (see page 24)
100g tomato, chopped
70g chopped onion
1 Scotch bonnet chilli, deseeded and very finely chopped
60ml olive oil
15g fresh coriander, chopped
sea salt and freshly ground black pepper

For Our Version of Bake
250g plain flour, plus more for rolling
1½ teaspoons baking powder
1 teaspoon sea salt
1½ teaspoons butter, cut into pieces
60ml water
5 tablespoons plus 1 teaspoon whole milk
475ml vegetable oil

Method

1 To make the salt fish, mix the salt fish with the tomato, onion and Scotch bonnet in a small heatproof bowl. Heat the oil in a small saucepan over a high heat. When very hot, pour the oil over the salt fish mixture. Add the coriander and season with sea salt and pepper. Leave to rest at room temperature for about 1 hour.

2 To make the bake, using a fine-mesh sieve, sift together the flour, baking powder and salt into a medium bowl. Rub the butter into the flour with your fingertips until well combined. Gradually add the water and milk and mix well with your hands until a dough is formed. Turn out onto a floured work surface and knead for about 5 minutes or until smooth.

3 Roll the dough into golf ball-sized pieces (you should get about eight in total) and leave to rest for about 30 minutes.

4 Heat the oil in a large saucepan over a high heat. Roll each dough ball out to a 10cm disc and score a line in the middle so that it cooks more quickly. Working in batches, fry the discs in the oil for about 2 minutes, turning over once. When the bakes float, they are ready. Place on a plate lined with kitchen paper to drain.

5 Serve the warm bakes with the salt fish. Refrigerate any leftover buljol for up to 2 days.

ACKEE AND BACON QUICHE

Here, we combine a traditional quiche custard with pure Jamaican love by adding our national fruit (and popular breakfast item), ackee, alongside crispy bacon. Throw in tons of flavour from the Scotch bonnet, spring onion, tomato, garlic, thyme and Parmesan cheese, and you have a winning brunch. If you don't have coconut milk to hand, use 360ml double cream instead of the cow's and coconut milk.

Makes 1 x 20cm quiche (serves 6–8)

For the Pastry Case and Custard
450g plain flour, plus more for rolling
pinch of sea salt
225g chilled butter, cut into pieces
up to 60ml iced water
240ml full-fat milk
120ml canned coconut milk
3 medium eggs
1 tablespoon Dijon mustard
dash of freshly grated nutmeg
sea salt

For the Ackee and Bacon Filling
2 tablespoons olive oil
2 tablespoons chopped onion
½ Scotch bonnet chilli, deseeded and very finely chopped
2 garlic cloves, very finely chopped
225g bacon rashers, finely chopped
2 tablespoons sliced spring onion
1 bunch fresh thyme, chopped
50g tomato, finely chopped
2 tablespoons finely chopped pepper
1 x 540g can ackee, drained
sea salt and freshly ground black pepper
100g Parmesan cheese, freshly grated

Method

1 Preheat the oven to 180°C/gas mark 4.

2 To make the pastry case, using a fine-mesh sieve, sift together the flour and the salt into a large bowl. Gently rub the butter into the flour with your fingertips until crumbly. Add just enough iced water to form a dough and knead until it comes together. Form into a ball, then, on a floured surface, roll the pastry dough into a round about 35cm in diameter. Transfer to a 20cm flan tin and press the pastry gently into the base and sides. Weigh down the pastry with raw rice on a piece of greaseproof paper and blind bake for 20 minutes. Remove the paper and rice and set on a wire rack to cool until ready to fill.

3 Meanwhile, to make the custard, put the milk, coconut milk, eggs, mustard and nutmeg in a medium bowl and whisk together thoroughly. Season with salt and pepper. Set aside until ready to bake.

4 To make the filling, heat the oil in a frying pan over a medium heat. Toss in the onion, Scotch bonnet and garlic and cook for about 5 minutes until softened. Add the bacon and sauté for about 5 minutes. Spoon off the excess fat, then stir in the spring onion, thyme, tomato and pepper and cook for 5 minutes or until the vegetables are tender. Add the ackee, season with salt and pepper and mix in the Parmesan. Leave to cool.

5 To assemble the quiche, place the ackee and bacon filling in the pastry case and smooth the top. Pour the custard over the filling, distributing it evenly with a fork. Return the quiche to the oven and bake for 45 minutes or until the custard has set. Leave to cool slightly before serving.

SMOKED MARLIN AND SALMON PLATTER WITH DILL CREAM CHEESE, LIME AND HARD-BOILED EGGS

A simple and sophisticated breakfast, brunch or lunch favourite, this lovely platter features smoked marlin (or trout), capers, marinated onions, dill cream cheese and boiled eggs. Accompany it with a baguette, bagels or our local toasted hardo bread and 'you gone clear' (you can't go wrong), as we say in Jamaica!

Serves 6

cream cheese, soured cream and dill mixture (page 56)

85g smoked marlin or smoked trout, thinly sliced

85g smoked salmon or gravadlax, thinly sliced

6 hard-boiled eggs, peeled

onion-caper relish (page 56)

2 limes, sliced

freshly ground black pepper

6 toasted or fresh bagels, baguette or, our favourite, toasted Jamaican hardo bread

Method

1 Mound the cream cheese mixture in the middle of a platter, then layer the marlin or trout on one side and the salmon or gravadlax on the other. Halve the eggs and place around the edge of the platter.

2 Sprinkle the onion-caper relish all over the salmon and marlin and scatter some lime slices on top. Sprinkle some pepper over all the ingredients on the platter and serve with the bagels or bread on the side.

PAN-ROASTED PUMPKIN, BACON AND GOAT'S CHEESE FRITTATA

Bursting with goodness, this frittata made even Suzanne, who hates eggs, go crazy! We love roasted pumpkin and goat's cheese, especially when it's warm and soft. Throw in some bacon, and it's a downright love affair of flavours for the palate! If calabaza pumpkin is not easy to find, feel free to use butternut squash.

Serves 4-6

1 tablespoon olive oil
225g bacon rashers, finely chopped
½ onion, chopped
1 garlic clove, diced
2 tablespoons chopped fresh thyme
450g calabaza pumpkin or butternut squash, peeled, deseeded and cut into 3mm-thick slices
6–8 medium eggs
1 teaspoon sea salt, plus more for seasoning
¼ teaspoon freshly ground black pepper, plus more for seasoning
55g chèvre (or other soft goat's cheese)
25g Parmesan cheese, freshly grated

Method

1 Preheat the oven on the grill setting, if you have one, or preheat the grill, with a shelf set 7.5–10cm from the heat source.

2 Place a 25cm non-stick ovenproof sauté pan over a medium heat. Add the oil and bacon and sauté until browned.

3 Transfer the bacon to a plate and set aside. Pour off most of the bacon fat into a small bowl and return the pan to the heat. Add the onion, garlic, and half the thyme and sauté for 2–3 minutes, then add the pumpkin or squash. Season with salt and pepper and sauté for about 5 minutes, adding more bacon fat if the pan gets too dry. Place the pan in the oven or under the grill and cook, uncovered, for about 15 minutes until the pumpkin or squash is soft.

4 In the meantime, whisk the eggs in a large bowl and add the remaining thyme, salt and pepper. Combine half the goat's cheese and Parmesan and whisk into the eggs.

5 Remove the pan from the oven or grill, pour the egg mixture in and stir with a spatula to make sure the egg gets underneath the pumpkin or squash. Dot the top with the remaining goat's cheese and cook over a medium heat, without stirring, for about 4 minutes until the egg mixture has set on the base and begins to set on top.

6 Sprinkle the top with the remaining Parmesan. Return the pan to the oven or grill for 3–4 minutes until the egg mixture is lightly browned and puffy. Loosen the frittata from the pan by moving a rubber spatula around the edges. Slide the frittata onto a plate or other serving dish and cut into six wedges. Serve warm or at room temperature.

10

SWEET FOR MY SWEET

DESSERTS AND SUGARY SNACKS

There is a great reggae song, the first line of which says: 'Sweet for my sweet and sugar for my honey', perfectly summing up the Jamaican love of all things sweet. Jamaica's dessert culture is a distinct blend of our British colonial influences (evidenced in the prevalence of puddings, trifles, buns and tarts) and more rustic preparations that are a product of our slave legacy. These indigenous desserts often combine basic ingredients like coconut, ginger, flour and sugar, as more expensive ingredients required for fancy desserts would not have been available to the average yeoman.

Coconut drops, peanut cake, grater cake, jack-ass corn (a traditional thin and crispy biscuit), Bustamante backbone (a gingery coconut boiled sweet), along with sweet potato, cassava and cornmeal pone are all examples of typical sweets inherited from our slave ancestors; all are still sold and consumed around the island to this day. In this chapter, we share recipes for a range of simple kitchen desserts, confectionery and baked goods that we feel aptly reflect the diversity of Caribbean desserts.

MANGA'S BREAD PUDDING

Manga, our paternal grandmother, was the baker of the family, and boy, could she bake! From puddings, to Easter buns, to patties and plantain tarts, she could do it all. She was well known for her bread pudding and we would often beg her to make us this treat whenever we visited. We modernise her family recipe by adding a coconut and rum crème anglaise. This is also delicious served warm served with rum and raisin ice cream (page 164).

Serves 10

12 medium eggs
950ml full-fat milk
120ml rum
½ teaspoon sea salt
2 teaspoons vanilla extract
2 teaspoons almond extract
4 teaspoons sugar
1 whole loaf Jamaican hardo bread, cut into
2.5cm cubes
85g raisins
4 teaspoons ground cinnamon
115g unsalted butter, melted
Coconut Rum Crème Anglaise, for serving
(page 160)

Method

1 Preheat the oven to 180°C/gas mark 4.

2 Whisk the eggs, milk, rum, salt, vanilla and almond extracts and 2 teaspoons of the sugar in a large bowl until the sugar is dissolved.

3 Place the cubed bread in a baking dish. Scatter with the raisins and sprinkle with 2 teaspoons of the cinnamon. Pour the milk mixture over the bread, then pour the melted butter on top. Sprinkle the top of the bread pudding with the remaining 2 teaspoons cinnamon and 2 teaspoons sugar.

4 Bake for 45 minutes until the pudding is set. Serve warm with the coconut run crème anglaise alongside.

CHOCOLATE COFFEE BREAD PUDDING

Coffee – especially Jamaica's own Blue Mountain coffee – and chocolate make perfect partners in a luscious bread pudding that we have served with great aplomb at Bellefield Great House in Montego Bay to rave reviews, over and over again.

Serves 12

12 medium eggs
700ml full-fat milk
250ml very strong brewed coffee
2 tablespoons rum
2 teaspoons vanilla extract
½ teaspoon sea salt
300g sugar, plus 2 teaspoons
1 whole loaf Jamaican hardo bread, cut into 2.5cm cubes
55g good-quality white baking chocolate, roughly chopped
55g good-quality dark chocolate, roughly chopped
4 teaspoons ground cinnamon
180g chocolate chips
115g butter, melted
3 tablespoons flaked almonds

Method

1 Preheat the oven to 180°C/gas mark 4.

2 Whisk together the eggs, milk, coffee, rum, vanilla, salt and the 300g sugar in a medium bowl until the sugar is dissolved.

3 Place the cubed bread in a baking dish. Scatter the white and dark chocolate pieces over the bread cubes and sprinkle with 2 teaspoons of the cinnamon.

4 Melt the chocolate chips in a heatproof bowl set over a saucepan of barely simmering water. Drizzle the melted chocolate over the bread. Pour the coffee and milk mixture on top, then the melted butter. Sprinkle the top of the bread pudding with the remaining 2 teaspoons cinnamon, 2 teaspoons sugar and the flaked almonds.

5 Bake for 45 minutes until the pudding is set. Serve warm.

MATRIMONY AMBROSIA

Matrimony is a Jamaican dessert that, as its name implies, is the marriage of two outstandingly distinctive fruits: the star apple, a milky purple fruit with a star at its centre when it's halved, and the most wonderful Jamaican orange, the ortanique, which is a hybrid of the tangerine and the Valencia orange. These two lovers are united by a bond of condensed milk in the traditional recipe for a match made in heaven. In our version, we make this divine pairing even more celestial by using a coconut rum crème anglaise instead.

Serves 8

For the Coconut Rum Crème Anglaise
475ml double cream
2 tablespoons red rum
50g coconut milk powder
180g icing sugar
60ml canned coconut milk

4 ortanique or navel oranges, peeled and segmented
4 star apples, peeled and cubed, or 165g each peeled and cored/stoned pineapple and mango, cubed
85g freshly grated coconut or shredded unsweetened dried coconut
100g pecan nuts, toasted and chopped

Method

1 To make the crème anglaise, put the cream, rum, coconut milk powder and icing sugar in the bowl of a stand mixer fitted with a whisk attachment and beat until stiff peaks form. Whisk in the coconut milk.

2 Combine the ortanique or orange segments, star apples or pineapple and mango and coconut in a mixing bowl. Stir in the crème anglaise. Transfer to a glass serving bowl, top with the pecans, cover with clingfilm and refrigerate for 2 hours before serving.

TÍA MARIA TIRAMISU

Tía Maria, a Jamaican coffee-based liqueur, and moist sponge cake are the highlights of this cool island-style tiramisu. One-third Tía Maria to two-thirds milk makes a delicious cocktail called a Brown Cow that we loved ordering at Devon House back in the day. We encourage you to try both the tiramisu and the Brown Cow; they are delightful creations for all coffee lovers.

Serves 12

5 medium egg yolks
250g sugar
1 teaspoon vanilla extract, plus 1 tablespoon
450g mascarpone cheese
475ml double cream
100g coconut milk powder
60ml rum
350ml chilled brewed coffee, preferably Blue Mountain
80ml Tía Maria (coffee liqueur)
1 x 15cm round ready-made sponge cake, sliced
115g dark chocolate, shaved

Method

1 Put the egg yolks in a mixing bowl and set it over a double boiler. Add 50g of the sugar and the 1 teaspoon vanilla and whisk until the yolks start to turn pale yellow. Cook over simmering water, scraping the sides of the bowl occasionally with a rubber spatula, until thick. Cover with clingfilm and refrigerate until cool.

2 Place the mascarpone in a bowl and stir until smooth.

3 Put the cream, coconut milk powder, the remaining 200g sugar and the rum in the bowl of a stand mixer fitted with a whisk attachment and whip until not quite stiff. Add the softened mascarpone and the chilled egg yolk mixture and fold gently together with a rubber spatula. Cover with clingfilm and refrigerate for 1 hour.

4 In another bowl, combine the coffee, Tía Maria and remaining 1 tablespoon vanilla. Arrange the slices of sponge cake in a single layer in a 23 x 33cm baking tin. Spoon a small amount of the coffee mixture over the cake. Plop a third of the coconut cream mixture on top and spread it into an even layer. Cover with a layer of shaved chocolate. Repeat the process two more times until you've used all the coffee mixture, coconut cream and shaved chocolate. Cover the tin with clingfilm and refrigerate for at least 2 hours before serving.

DALTON'S PLANTAIN TARTS

Dalton is our amazing chef at Bellefield Great House in Montego Bay, and he has a wealth of experience, good vibes and good food. His recipe, which we share here, for the typical Jamaican sweet treat, plantain tarts, is sensational! We fold the pastry like a turnover, enclosing the traditionally red-coloured filling of very ripe sweet plantains.

Makes 12 hand pies

For the Pastry
450g plain flour, plus more for rolling
1 teaspoon sea salt
225g cold butter, cut into 1cm pieces
up to 4 tablespoons iced water

For the Filling
3 very ripe (black) plantains
50g granulated sugar
2 teaspoons vanilla extract
1 teaspoon freshly grated nutmeg
2 teaspoons red food colouring
1 egg white, beaten
30g icing sugar, for dusting

Method

1 To make the pastry, using a fine-mesh sieve, sift the flour and salt together into a medium bowl. Rub in the butter with your fingertips until well incorporated and the mixture appears sandy in texture. Stir in the iced water until a dough forms, then knead on a work surface for a few turns to bring the dough together. Tightly wrap the dough in clingfilm and chill for 3 hours in the fridge.

2 Meanwhile, to make the filling, peel the plantains and cut into pieces. Place in a small saucepan with enough water to cover and bring to the boil, then simmer for 5–10 minutes, depending on how ripe the plantains are, until tender. Once soft, pour out the water and mash the plantains with the granulated sugar, vanilla, nutmeg and food colouring. Set aside to cool.

3 When ready to bake, preheat the oven to 180°C/gas mark 4.

4 Roll out the dough on a lightly floured surface to about 5mm thick. Cut the dough into a dozen 10–13cm rounds. Spoon a little of the plantain filling into the centre of each round, then fold in half to form a crescent shape. Press the edges together with a fork and place the pies on a baking tray. Slice a small hole in the top of each pie to act as an air vent, brush with the egg white and sprinkle with the icing sugar. Bake for 20–25 minutes until golden brown.

5 Leave the pies to cool to room temperature before serving.

COCONUT DROPS

On a recent visit to New Orleans for Michelle's presentation on traditional Jamaican confectionery and Jamaican candy ladies at the New Orleans's Historic Collection and Dillard University, we met Leah Chase, the chef/owner of New Orleans's Dooky Chase Restaurant (the first African American-owned fine dining restaurant in the USA). She said her grandmother explained that pralines were originally made with coconut before they were made with pecans. All of our traditional Jamaican sweets are made with coconut and, no doubt, these similarities are not a coincidence, but date back to the shared heritage of slavery, African ancestors and the plantation systems in both the Caribbean islands and the American South. Here is our recipe for coconut drops, which are made with just four basic ingredients. Give 'em a try – they are easy and tasty!

Makes 12–16 drops

1 whole medium mature coconut
5–6 tablespoons peeled and very finely chopped fresh ginger
475ml water
630g dark brown sugar
1 large banana leaf (or use a sheet of greased greaseproof paper)

Method

1 Using a hammer, break the coconut and remove the hard outer shell. Using a small knife, dice the hard coconut flesh into small cubes.

2 Combine the coconut and ginger in a bowl, then place in a saucepan. Add the water and brown sugar to the coconut and bring to the boil over a high heat.

3 Reduce the heat to medium and cook, stirring frequently, for 1 hour 45 minutes–2 hours, until the water has evaporated and the sugar is caramelised and sticky.

4 Place a large banana leaf or a sheet of greased greaseproof paper on a kitchen work surface. Drop spoonfuls of the coconut mixture on the banana leaf or paper and let them cool and harden before serving. These keep for up to 1 week.

HOMEMADE ICE CREAM

Rum and raisin, coconut, coffee and stout are, without a doubt, the bestselling flavours for Jamaican ice cream. Jamaican rum and raisin ice cream is distinctive because we have fantastic rum; the same can be said for our local coffee ice cream. In Jamaica, you'll also find a wide range of atypical ice cream flavours: sour sop, guava, grape nut, prune, fruit and nut, pineapple and mango are all regularly available and in demand on Sundays, which is 'ice cream day' for many families across the island. The recipes that follow are reminiscent in flavour to our infamous Devon House Ice Cream in Kingston.

RUM AND RAISIN ICE CREAM

Makes about 475ml

100g sugar, or less to taste
1 tablespoon plus 1 teaspoon cornflour
⅛ teaspoon sea salt
410ml canned evaporated milk
240ml double cream
1 medium egg yolk
1½ teaspoons vanilla extract
120ml red rum
40g raisins

Method

1 Combine the sugar, cornflour and salt in a large, heavy-based saucepan. Gradually whisk in the evaporated milk and cream and cook over a medium heat, stirring constantly, for 10–12 minutes or until the mixture thickens slightly. Remove from the heat.

2 Whisk the egg yolk in a small bowl until slightly thickened. Temper the yolk by gradually whisking about 250ml of the hot cream mixture into the yolk, then add the yolk mixture to the remaining cream mixture in the saucepan, whisking constantly. Whisk in the vanilla and 60ml of the rum. Cool for 1 hour, stirring occasionally.

3 Place clingfilm directly on the surface of the cream mixture and chill for 8–24 hours.

4 Soak the raisins in the remaining 60ml rum and refrigerate for at least 3 hours or overnight. Drain any excess liquid from the raisins and stir the raisins into the chilled cream mixture.

5 Pour the mixture into the container of a 1.5-litre electric ice cream maker and then freeze according to the manufacturer's instructions.

COCONUT ICE CREAM

Makes about 475ml

100g sugar
1 tablespoon plus 1 teaspoon cornflour
⅛ teaspoon sea salt
475ml canned coconut milk
240ml double cream
1 medium egg yolk
1½ teaspoons vanilla extract
20g shredded unsweetened dried coconut (optional)

Method

1 Combine the sugar, cornflour and salt in a large, heavy-based saucepan. Gradually whisk in the coconut milk and cream and cook over a medium heat, stirring constantly, for 10–12 minutes or until the mixture thickens slightly. Remove from the heat.

2 Whisk the egg yolk in a small bowl until slightly thickened. Temper the yolk by gradually whisking about 250ml of the hot cream mixture into the yolk, then add the yolk mixture to the remaining cream mixture in the saucepan, whisking constantly. Stir in the vanilla and coconut, if using. Cool for 1 hour, stirring occasionally.

3 Place clingfilm directly on the surface of the ice cream mixture and chill for 8–24 hours.

4 Pour the mixture into the container of a 1.5-litre electric ice cream maker and then freeze according to the manufacturer's instructions.

COFFEE ICE CREAM

Makes about 475ml

100g sugar
1 tablespoon plus 1 teaspoon cornflour
⅛ teaspoon sea salt
240ml canned evaporated milk
240ml double cream
1 medium egg yolk
1½ teaspoons vanilla extract
240ml extra-strong freshly brewed coffee
80g chocolate-covered coffee beans (optional)

Method

1 Put the sugar, cornflour and salt in a large, heavy-based saucepan. Gradually whisk in the evaporated milk and cream and cook over a medium heat, stirring constantly, for 10–12 minutes or until the mixture thickens slightly. Remove from the heat.

2 Whisk the egg yolk in a small bowl until slightly thickened. Temper the yolk by gradually whisking about 250ml of the hot cream mixture into the egg yolk, then add the yolk mixture to the remaining cream mixture in the saucepan, whisking constantly. Stir in the vanilla and coffee and continue whisking for about 5 minutes until well combined. Cool for 1 hour, stirring occasionally.

3 Place clingfilm directly on the surface of the ice cream mixture and chill for 8–24 hours. Just before adding to the ice cream machine, stir in the coffee beans, if using.

4 Pour the mixture into the container of a 1.5-litre electric ice cream maker and then freeze according to manufacturer's instructions.

STOUT ICE CREAM

Makes about 475ml

300ml stout
100g sugar
1 tablespoon plus 1 teaspoon cornflour
⅛ teaspoon sea salt
240ml evaporated milk
180ml double cream
1 medium egg yolk
1½ teaspoons vanilla extract

Method

1 Warm the stout over a medium heat in a small saucepan. Add 50g of the sugar and whisk until melted. Set aside.

2 Put the remaining sugar, the cornflour and salt in a large, heavy-based saucepan. Gradually whisk in the evaporated milk and cream over a medium heat, stirring constantly, for 10–12 minutes or until the mixture thickens slightly. Remove from the heat.

3 Whisk the egg yolk in a small bowl until slightly thickened. Temper the yolk by gradually whisking 250ml of the cream mixture into the yolk. Then add the yolk and cream mixture back into the remaining cream mixture in the saucepan, whisking constantly. Whisk in the vanilla and the stout mixture. Cool for 1 hour, stirring occasionally.

4 Place clingfilm directly on the surface of the ice cream mixture and chill for 8–24 hours.

5 Pour the mixture into the container of a 1.5-litre electric ice cream maker and then freeze according to manufacturer's instructions.

CRÊPES À LA MODE WITH FLAMBÉED BANANAS AND WARM ORTANIQUE RUM SAUCE

To flambé safely at home, make sure that you have a metal cover handy that is large enough to tightly fit your saucepan. That way if the flame becomes too large you can control the flame by cutting off the oxygen. Slightly warming the alcohol by placing it in a pan of recently boiled water will make the flame catch more quickly. Add in the scoop of ice cream (we like coconut), and this dessert is just deeevine!

Serves 8–10

For the Crêpes
3 medium eggs
350ml milk
1½ tablespoons rum
125g plain flour
½ teaspoon sea salt
85g butter, melted

For the Flambéed Bananas
50g brown sugar
45g butter, at room temperature
½ teaspoon ground cinnamon
60ml ortanique or orange juice
6 bananas, diagonally sliced
60ml Grand Marnier or Cointreau
3 tablespoons Appleton Estate rum (or other dark rum)

60ml ortanique or orange juice
1 tablespoon grated ortanique or orange zest
10 tablespoons icing sugar
130g butter, at room temperature
3 tablespoons Appleton Estate rum (or other dark rum)
ortanique or navel orange segments, for serving
vanilla ice cream or Coconut Ice Cream (page 164), for serving

Method

1 To make crêpes, whisk together the eggs, milk and rum in a medium bowl. Add the flour and salt and beat until smooth – the batter should be slightly thick, but still liquid in consistency. Refrigerate for about 30 minutes or up to 2 hours.

2 To make the flambéed bananas, melt the brown sugar, butter and cinnamon in a large saucepan over a medium heat until the sugar is melted and bubbling. Whisk in the ortanique juice and reduce for about 3 minutes. Add the bananas and sauté until softened and beginning to brown. Pour the Grand Marnier or Cointreau over the bananas and cook for about 2 minutes until evaporated. Splash with the rum and light with a match, allowing the rum to burn off. Set aside off the heat.

3 Simmer the ortanique or orange juice and zest with the icing sugar in a medium saucepan over a medium heat for about 5 minutes until reduced by half. Whisk in the butter, a little at a time. Add the rum just before serving; in the meantime, keep warm or set aside at room temperature.

4 Heat a crêpe pan over a medium heat and brush with some melted butter. Pour about 3 tablespoons batter into the pan, swirling to spread it around evenly. Cook until the underside is golden, then flip over and cook for about another 1 minute until the other side is golden. Transfer to a plate and keep warm.

5 Fill the crêpes with the flambéed bananas and roll up like a burrito. Cut diagonally in half and top with the ortanique or orange segments and ice cream. Add the rum to the rum sauce, pour over the crêpes and serve.

CARAMELISED BANANA AND COCONUT CRÈME BRÛLÉE

Crème brûlée is one of Michelle's favourite desserts, and this one is 'nice cyant done', meaning that the niceness cannot end. The addition of coconut, banana and nutmeg gives this classic French dish an island twist. We have served it at various events with great success, one of which was the official dinner for HRH the Prince of Wales at Jamaica House when he visited in 2008.

Serves 12

Flambéed Bananas (page 166)
475ml double cream
240ml coconut milk
2 teaspoons vanilla extract
1 teaspoon freshly grated nutmeg
6 medium egg yolks
9 tablespoons sugar

Method

1 Preheat the oven to 165°C/gas mark 3.

2 Divide the flambéed bananas between six wide, shallow crème brûlée dishes or 175ml ramekins and leave to cool.

3 Put the cream and coconut milk in a medium saucepan. Add the vanilla and nutmeg and bring the cream just to the boil, then remove from the heat and set aside.

4 Put the egg yolks and 5 tablespoons of the sugar in a stainless-steel bowl over a saucepan of boiling water. Whisk the egg yolks and sugar together, and then stir over the simmering water for about 15 minutes until the mixture becomes fairly thick. Add the cream mixture to the egg mixture, and continue to whisk over the double boiler for about 10 minutes until it forms a custard.

5 Ladle the custard over the cooled flambéed bananas in the six dishes. Place the dishes in a roasting tin and fill the pan with enough hot water to come halfway up the sides of the dishes. Bake for 40 minutes or until the custards are set in the centre. Remove the dishes from the pan and chill for at least 3 hours.

6 When you are ready to serve, sprinkle about 2 teaspoons sugar over each custard, distributing it evenly. Place the ramekins under a hot grill until the sugar caramelises, or heat with a kitchen blow torch. Serve while the crust is still hot.

EASY NO-BAKE GINGER LYCHEE TRIFLE

Trifle is a common dessert in the Caribbean during the holiday season, and is admittedly very British in origin. Because of our colonial past, many of our food influences came from the so-called mother land, and the tradition of Christmas trifle is one of them. This easy version, which uses a shop-bought rum cake as its base, was inspired by an incredible trifle we ate one night at the Guilt Trip Restaurant in Kingston, and the supreme talent of its chef/owner and fellow foodie, Colin Hylton. Colin's innovative use of local fruits and ingredients in his dessert creations are nothing short of extraordinary. His culinary creations, both sweet and savoury, define modern Caribbean cuisine at its most glorious.

Serves 12

2 teaspoons Bird's custard powder
240ml coconut milk
240ml double cream
3 tablespoons sugar
1 powdered ginger tea sachet
2 teaspoons peeled and grated fresh ginger
1 small shop-bought rum cake (or sponge or Madeira cake drizzled with rum), split horizontally into 3 layers
60ml ortanique or orange juice
30g flaked almonds, toasted
2 ortaniques or navel oranges, peeled and segmented
1 x 425g can lychees, drained and sliced (liquid reserved)

For the Drunken Whipped Cream

120ml double cream
2 tablespoons sugar
1 teaspoon rum

Method

1 Put the custard powder in a small bowl. Warm the coconut milk, cream and sugar in a saucepan, stirring until the sugar is dissolved. Pour the hot cream mixture over the custard powder and whisk until the custard begins to thicken. Add the powdered ginger tea and grated ginger and whisk to combine. Set aside to cool.

2 To make the drunken whipped cream, put the cream, sugar and rum in the bowl of a stand mixer fitted with a whisk attachment and whisk until stiff peaks form.

3 To assemble the trifle, place a layer of cake in the base of a glass bowl, top generously with one-third of the ginger custard, drizzle with ortanique or orange juice and sprinkle with almonds. Add one-third of the ortanique or orange segments and lychees, top with another layer of rum cake, pour over another third of the ginger custard and 60ml lychee juice and top with almonds, lychees and oranges. Add the final layer of cake, followed by the remaining third of the custard and juice and topped with the rest of the fruit. Top with the drunken whipped cream and a sprinkle of almonds. Refrigerate for at least 2 hours before serving.

INGREDIENT NOTE

Powdered ginger tea, which is already sweetened, can be purchased at a Caribbean food shop or market, or online; see our Resources section on page 186.

LEMON PASSION FRUIT SQUARES

Sweet yet tart and definitely 'moreish', or addictive, this harmonious mixture of lemon and lime with a twist of passion fruit is, in a word, blissful! Here is our Caribbean take on the typical lemon square.

Makes 12

For the Base

225g unsalted butter, at room temperature
100g sugar
250g plain flour, plus more for dusting
⅛ teaspoon sea salt

6 large eggs, at room temperature
600g granulated sugar
120ml fresh lemon juice
60ml fresh lime juice
2 tablespoons grated lime zest
125g plain flour
65g passion fruit pulp
icing sugar, for dusting

Method

1 To make the base, put the butter and sugar in the bowl of a stand mixer fitted with a paddle attachment and beat for 8–10 minutes until light and fluffy. Using a fine-mesh sieve, sift the flour and salt together into a medium bowl. With the mixer on low, gradually add the flour to the butter mixture and blend until just combined.

2 Dump the dough onto a well-floured surface and gather it into a mass. Flour your hands well and use the tips of your fingers to press the dough into a 23 x 33cm baking tin, building up a 1cm edge on all sides. Chill for about 30 minutes until the base has set.

3 Preheat the oven to 180°C/gas mark 4. Bake the base for about 20 minutes until lightly browned. Leave it to cool completely but keep the oven on.

4 Whisk together the eggs, granulated sugar, lemon juice, lime juice and zest and flour in a large bowl. Mix in the passion fruit pulp, pour the filling over the cooled base and bake for 40–50 minutes until the filling is set. Leave to cool completely before dusting with icing sugar, cutting into squares and serving.

BRAWTA

A LITTLE SOMETHING EXTRA

Brawta is patois for 'a little something extra'. For example, say you're buying fruit from a street-side fruit vendor in a very busy part of Kingston, and you want a dozen of the sweetest Bombay mangos. Because you are a good customer, the fruit vendor will give you 13 mangos instead of 12. The 13th mango is your 'brawta', a little something extra from the vendor to show his or her appreciation for your patronage. (And, if you've ever tasted a Bombay mango, you would be thrilled to have an extra!) Sometimes a customer will ask for a brawta.

Probably a vestige of the old bartering system used for the exchange of goods and services, brawta is still alive and well today, especially when at the market or when buying from smaller produce vendors. So, here is our brawta for you – some special, extra recipes from our restaurant menus and many years of catering and event planning. We hope that these drinks and party snacks, decorating ideas and tips for easy entertaining will help you round out your fetin' time in true Caribbean style.

THIRST QUENCHERS: THE BASIC CARIBBEAN BAR

Whenever we think of drinks, we think of our grandfather, Hugh Holness, aka Gampi. Rum and water was his drink of choice, and we were allowed little sips at a young age to introduce our palates to the taste of fine rum. Gampi was a man who knew how to make a drink; we would bombard him with requests for a Jamaican-style ice cream soda or a Horlicks milkshake with a splash of rum and he would usually oblige. So, we dedicate this little section on the Caribbean bar to our Gampi, with whom we shared many a good drink. As he would say, 'Cin cin', or cheers! If you are not into fancy cocktails or just can't be bothered to mix them, don't fret – just put our basic Caribbean bar together and let your guests serve themselves. Here is a list of what you need to get the party started. (You'll see that it is heavy on the rum!)

CARIBBEAN BAR ESSENTIALS

Red Stripe beer / Red Stripe Light (Jamaica's favourite beer)
Carib beer (Trinidad's favourite beer)
Rum cream liqueur (Wray & Nephew or Sangster's)
Angostura bitters
Tía Maria (a Jamaican coffee liqueur; a good alternative is Kahlúa)
Coconut rum (try Sangster's or Wray & Nephew)
Red rum (good-quality options are Appleton, Mount Gay, Angostura and Demerara)
White overproof rum (Wray & Nephew)
Tropical fruit juices (like guava, mango and pineapple)
Ginger ale or ginger beer
Ting (a delicious Jamaican grapefruit soda)
Shandy (you can make your own using 1 part beer to 1 part ginger ale or ginger beer)
Plenty of fresh limes
Coconut water

1-2-3-4 PUNCH: THE ONLY COCKTAIL RECIPE YOU'LL EVER NEED

We like very simple cocktails, and most times can't even be bothered to make those. But if we have to make one, we always fall back on a version of this 'no fail' 1-2-3-4 punch. It's easy, quick and simple; better yet, it always works!

The recipe goes something like this:
1 of sour
2 of sweet
3 of strong
4 of weak

So, here's how it works in practice:
240ml lemon juice or 1 part of something sour
420g brown sugar or 2 parts of something sweet (like honey, simple syrup or agave)
700ml white rum or 3 parts of something strong – i.e. vodka or red rum
950ml water or 4 parts of a chaser (like soda water or juice)

Mix together all the ingredients in a pitcher, pour into your glass of choice, settle back (preferably on a lounge chair) and sip away! Chill and serve over ice with a lime or orange garnish.

FETIN' 101:
HOW TO THROW AN ISLAND PARTY

In the Caribbean, we have a unique style of entertaining. Our parties are notorious for great music, crazy dancing, an abundance of food and booze and incredibly happy vibes. If that sounds good to you and you want to try 'keeping' (Jamaican slang for hosting or throwing) a party, here is a list of simple guidelines that we always follow:

Never overplan: last-minute fetes are always the best!
We love party crashers – they bring new energy to a party and make it really swing. But, as a general rule, they should be familiar or known to you, like friends of friends. Our policy when it comes to feting is the more the merrier!

Keep it simple. Focus on the important elements: great music, easy food, plenty of drink, lots of dancing. For larger events, make the dance floor the centre focus with the bar and food surrounding it. This lets your guests see what is going on and feel the energy from the dance floor.

For a large fete, ditch the chairs and categorically no dining tables – even if you're serving food. We eat standing because we are usually dancing at the same time! If you do want to provide seating and tables, set up some casual seating away from the main party area. Sofas, outdoor benches and high-top tables informally grouped together are a great way to create less traditional dining and seating areas. Loud music is essential at a Caribbean dance party.

Have a diverse guest list. The Caribbean is known for its cultural diversity, and people of all ages always party

together. Invite that one group of people who love to dance even if they aren't your best friends. In the Caribbean we have 'feting friends' who we only see when we are out, but who are great fun at a party.

Keep the alcohol and food flowing!
Caribbean people have a fear of running out of anything; the drinks and party food don't have to be expensive, but it must never run out!

Warm up your guests with a strong welcome drink: our 1-2-3-4 Punch with rum (page 176) is perfect for this!

If you are having over 40 guests, splurge on a bartender or two – preferably one that can dance (Caribbean bartenders always dance to the music while they serve). The rule of thumb to follow is to have one bartender for every 20–30 guests.

PARTY LINGO

In the Caribbean, we take our entertaining very seriously and have designated names for all types of events. Here are a few you will hear us throwing around a lot. All serious party people should take note.

LYME (Trini) = A casual get-together, not too large and usually thrown together at the last minute. Includes some music and dancing, or a group of people simply 'lyming' (or hanging out). Also used as a verb.

FETE (Trini) = A large dance party with massive speaker boxes, a professional DJ and non-stop dancing and drinking, varying from 150 guests up to 2,000 or more. In our part of the world, fetes usually go on until the sun comes up. We also have day fetes, which start at about midday and carry on until dark. Also used as a verb: 'to fete', meaning to party. In Jamaica, a fete is referred to as a 'session' or 'bashment'.

DANCE = A street dance party where a DJ, or 'sound', sets up huge speakers outside of a bar, on the pavement or in the town square. The speakers usually face the road and blast dancehall music and slow jams all night long. A dance is open to all, so residents and passerbys often stop to buy a drink (stout is the drink of choice), listen to some 'tunes' and 'hole a cotch by a speaker box' (hang out by the speakers). From Friday evening right through to the wee hours of Monday morning, and on most public holidays (usually starting at about 6pm), there is a dance in full swing in many communities across the island.

GET-TOGETHER = Like a lyme, a small informal gathering of friends, hanging out and catching up on life; usually drinks and snacks make up the menu, with some sweet island music in the background.

MASS = Carnival Day in any island culminates with a 'mass' or 'road march', which is an all-day street party starting at about 8am and going on until dark. Revellers dress in costumes and 'play mass' through the streets, 'chipping', or dancing, behind music trucks that blast both live and recorded soca music at unbelievably high decibels. Copious amounts of alcohol are consumed, coupled with bacchanalian dancing. For the carnival lover, this is truly a spiritual experience!

COOK UP (Jamaican) = Cook up, or 'running a boat', as we say in Jamaica, is when a group gets together to cook a meal to share. It is a form of socialising, but also a way of saving money. It is common practice on construction sites for the men to run a boat at lunchtime.

BLOCKO (Trini) = A 'blocko' party hails from Trinidad and is similar to a block party in the USA. A road, usually in a private community, is blocked off on both ends to set up a fete. The entire street is the dance floor, and all the required elements for a Caribbean party are in full display – DJs, loud music, gigantic speaker boxes, lots of booze, good vibes and dancing.

THREE THINGS EVERY CATERER KNOWS

There are certain basic truths that every caterer, chef or restaurant owner knows to be self-evident. Without these truths, we would not be able to produce food for such large quantities of people with such apparent ease. Essentially, it's all about being prepared. While there are many tips that we could share, we consider these three simple pointers to be the most important in the hectic world of today – particularly if you do a lot of home cooking and entertaining.

1. Prep and Hold

Organisation is, simply put, the most important aspect in hosting a successful event, no matter how large or small. Make lists, because a list can save your life. It's a sign of a great hostess, and a sign of respect for your guests, to be ready, organised and calm when you host a party. There is simply nothing worse than arriving at a dinner party to find chaos and mess; it makes you feel like you've arrived too early. A good hostess is always ready for her guests – and even if she isn't, they should never know!

In the event business, when it comes to food, we get organised by preparing all our food items to a certain point and then holding them for service. At service time (or closer to it), we 'finish' the items so that the food is as fresh as possible.

Here's an example of what we would do if we had a few friends coming over for a pasta dinner:
• Prep everything and get it ready for serving:
>   make the pasta sauce and hold
>   grate the Parmesan

- Clean up the kitchen:
  - wash everything and clean all surface mess
- Lay out all your serving utensils:
  - set the table
  - put on some music
  - add ambiance like flowers and candles
- Get dressed and have a glass of wine while you wait for your guests! When your guests arrive, you will be relaxed and looking fabulous – and you can get your meal ready in as little as 20 minutes!

2. Batch Sauces and Dressings

One of the best ways to make sure you always have a tasty home-cooked meal is by batch-preparing certain items. Many marinades, vinaigrettes, sauces and chutneys can be kept for extended periods of time (sometimes up to three weeks in the fridge, or more). When you make big batches of basic sauces and dressings and keep them on hand, whipping together a quick meal is easy and hassle-free.

Here are some items we are sure to have in our fridge at all times: Scotch Bonnet Oil, Spicy West Indian Salsa Verde, Coffee Jerked Seasoning, Honey Balsamic Salad Dressing, Papaya Dipping Sauce and Peanut Coconut Dipping Sauce, to name a few, all of which are in this book! These items are so tasty that they can be used with a variety of different dishes. For the home cook, batching items saves both time and money – and allows you to have a gourmet meal ready in minutes, any time at all.

3. Marinate and Portion Meat

The best thing you can do to speed up the cooking and preparation process is to prep meat in bulk, seal in individually portioned bags, date and freeze. This is not just for big dinner parties. If you live alone or have a small family, a useful tip for easy home-cooked meals in minutes is to simply marinate and portion bulk meat, poultry or fish into individual servings right after you purchase it and freeze them in separate resealable plastic bags. The portions of meat can easily be left to defrost in the fridge during the day, making dinner a few quick minutes away. And if you've followed our above advice, you should have a nice selection of fresh sauces, marinades, chutneys and salsas on hand to give your meal an extra-special twist.

SIX SIMPLE DÉCOR TIPS FOR A TABLE

We have decorated, styled and coordinated many parties during our years in the event and catering business. Over time, we have gathered some great ideas that will quickly enhance your table for any type of event with panache and ease.

- Use an eclectic mix of chairs, place settings and glassware, blending contemporary with antique pieces.
- Use colourful or patterned fabric ends to make gorgeous runners, napkins and tablecloths. Don't be afraid to mix colour and patterns, as it makes a party come alive.
- Always use candles and lanterns in varying shapes and sizes to create atmosphere for evening parties. They add natural light and warmth on the dining table and throughout the party space.
- Use unique vessels and props to hold flowers, like teapots, cups and glasses.
- Try submerging tropical flowers and/or leaves in water in tall, clear glass cylinders – they are a modern and unusual alternative to typical flower arrangements in vases. Using tropical fruits in this way is also very attractive and sophisticated.
- Create different heights on your buffet table by using risers or blocks – it makes the buffet dramatic and stylish. When dressing your buffet table, create a central focus in the middle of the table – a fantastic arrangement of flowers or a piece of sculpture.

A DOZEN SUPER-EASY RECIPES FOR LAST-MINUTE ENTERTAINING

There are always going to be those times when you suddenly find yourself with unexpected visitors that you need to feed; maybe your girlfriends decide to drop by for a cup of tea or a glass of wine, and you have nothing prepared. Fear not. Here are super-easy recipes – both savoury and sweet – that will get you out of any last-minute entertaining binds. All can be made in just 5–10 minutes. (Seriously!)

CREAM CHEESE AND PEPPER JELLY

Serves 8

225g cream cheese
175g hot pepper jelly from a jar
1 packet good-quality water crackers (such as Excelsior – see page 15)

Place the cream cheese on a plate. Pour the pepper jelly over the cream cheese and let it drip down the sides. Surround with the water crackers and then serve.

CREAM CHEESE AND SOLOMON GUNDY DIP

Serves 8–10

225g cream cheese
1 teaspoon fresh lime juice
1 handful chopped spring onions
175g Solomon Gundy from a jar
1 packet good-quality water crackers (such as Excelsior – see page 15)

Blend the cream cheese, lime juice, spring onions and Solomon Gundy in a food processor, or mix by hand. Transfer to a pretty bowl and serve with water crackers.

BANANA AND MANCHEGO FLATBREAD

Serves 8

2 x 15–20cm ready-made flatbreads or pitta breads
2 tablespoons banana chutney
85g Manchego cheese, shaved or grated
3 tablespoons sliced black olives
sea salt and freshly ground black pepper
1 handful fresh mint leaves
2 teaspoons olive oil

Preheat your grill. Place the breads on a baking tray and spread each with 1 tablespoon chutney, top with the cheese and olives, season with salt and pepper and sprinkle with the mint leaves. Drizzle with the oil and grill for 3–5 minutes until crispy. Cut each bread into eight pieces and serve.

GOAT'S CHEESE AND PAPAYA CHUTNEY WITH CRACKERS, DRIED FRUITS AND NUTS

Serves 6–8

1 x 225g log soft goat's cheese
125g papaya chutney or chutney of choice
assorted dried fruit like dates and apricots
assorted nuts
assorted crackers

Place the log of goat's cheese on a platter or cheese board. Serve with small bowls of the chutney, dried fruit, nuts and crackers.

BACON-WRAPPED PLANTAIN GLAZED WITH HONEY

Serves 6

12 x 5cm cubes fried ripe plantain (can be made ahead and held)
6 bacon rashers, cut in half
12 teaspoons honey
wooden cocktail sticks

Preheat your grill. Take the cubes of fried ripe plantain and wrap each with a strip of bacon. Secure with a cocktail stick and place on a baking tray. Drizzle each plaintain cube with 1 teaspoon honey and grill for 5–8 minutes until the bacon is caramelised and sticky, then serve immediately.

GRAPEFRUIT AND HONEY

Serves 2

1 medium grapefruit
about 2 tablespoons honey, preferably
Jamaican

Cut the grapefruit in half and remove
the centre core with all the seeds. With
a paring knife, cut out the grapefruit
segments and place in two small bowls.
Drizzle with the honey and serve to a
surprise breakfast visitor.

BOMBAY MANGO ICE CREAM

Serves 2-4

2 Bombay (or other) mangos
4 x 85g scoops Coconut Ice Cream
(page 164)

Slice the mangos crossways with a
sharp knife. Twist both sides in
opposite directions to open the mango.
Remove the stone and place both
halves in bowls in the fridge to chill.
Serve chilled, with a scoop of coconut
ice cream in the centre, for an
amazing but simple dessert.

HOMEMADE ICE CREAM SANDWICHES ON GINGER SNAPS

Serves 6

6 x 55g scoops of Rum and Raisin Ice
Cream (page 164)
12 Jamaican ginger biscuits
40g peanuts, crushed

Sandwich a scoop of ice cream
between two ginger biscuits. Repeat
with the rest of the ice cream and
ginger biscuits, then roll the ice
cream edges in the peanuts. Wrap in
clingfilm and place in the freezer
for 30 minutes before serving as a
delicious snack or easy dessert for
a barbecue.

BAKED BANANAS WITH CHOCOLATE AND COCONUT ICE CREAM

Serves 6

6 bananas, peeled and sliced lengthways
1 x 100g bar milk chocolate, preferably
Cadbury's, shaved
6 scoops Coconut Ice Cream (page 164)
or your flavour of choice

Place each banana on a piece of
foil on a baking tray. Top with the
chocolate and close up the foil to
create individual parcels. Bake in
the oven or on the barbecue for
20 minutes. Open the foil and serve
with a scoop of ice cream on top.

COCONUT WITH BROWN SUGAR

Serves 6-8

1 whole mature coconut, fleshy insides
removed (see page 24)
3 tablespoons brown sugar

Slice the firm coconut meat into
thick pieces. Arrange on a platter and
sprinkle with brown sugar. Serve for a
great snack.

OUR MANGO CHOW

Serves 6-8

475ml distilled white vinegar
1 Scotch bonnet chilli, cut into slices,
or hot pepper sauce to taste
1 teaspoon sea salt
freshly ground black pepper
½ teaspoon sugar (optional)
4 not-quite-ripe mangos, or pineapple,
June plum (see page 18) or any firm
tropical fruit, peeled, stoned/cored
and sliced

Stir together the vinegar, Scotch
bonnet, salt, pepper and sugar, if
using, in a large bowl. Add the mango
or other tropical fruit slices and
macerate for about 30 minutes until
the vinegar is well absorbed into the
fruit. Serve.

SHOPPING FOR CARIBBEAN INGREDIENTS

There is a wealth of Caribbean food shops, supermarkets and street markets across the UK that sell all kinds of Caribbean products, making it easy to find many of the ingredients we suggest in our recipes. For our readers' shopping convenience, we have listed some of the more well-known ones below; see our website for further suggestions.

Food Shops and Markets
Authentic Jamaican Foodstore (Birmingham)
Options Supermarket (Birmingham)
Brixton Market (Brixton, London)
Choumert Road Market (Peckham, London)
Deptford Market (Deptford, London)
Hildreth Street Market (Balham, London)
Lewisham Market (Lewisham, London)
Tooting Market (Tooting, London)

Online Caribbean Food Suppliers
Grace Foods: caribbeanfoodcentre. com
afrocaribbeanstore.co.uk
theasiancookshop.co.uk/caribbean-food-online-59-c.asp
africart-online.co.uk

CARIBBEAN BRANDS WE REALLY LOVE

To add extra sweet island flavour to every meal, we encourage you to sample any or all of these amazing Caribbean purveyors for a wide selection of preserves, chutneys, sauces, canned goods, condiments and the best Jamaican patties you will ever eat.

Belcour Preserves: Homemade artisan preserves and chutneys made from old family recipes. The tomato chutney and mixed fruit chutney are faves of ours. belcourpreserves.com

Busha Browne: An exotic and unique selection of chutneys, pepper sauces, jams and jellies. We love the pepper jelly, banana chutney, burnt orange marmalade and pukka pepper sauce. bushabrowne.com

Eaton's: A purveyor of a small selection of chutneys and preserves; they make an amazing papaya chutney that we just love, especially with goat's cheese. eatonsjamaica.net

Golden Krust Patties: A well-known patty franchise in the USA, they also serve a selection of other traditional Jamaican foods. goldenkrustbakery.com

Grace Foods: Distributes an extensive selection of Caribbean food products of all kinds – like canned ackee, coconut milk and beans – available throughout the UK in supermarkets and through their online stores. We love the Grace guava jelly and Grace pepper sauce (which is a bit like Tabasco). gracefoods.co.uk

Great House Preserves: A newer company with a small but lovely selection of jams and jellies.

Juici Beef Patties: Jamaica's other number one patty (it's a tie with Tastee Patties). juicipatties.com

Linstead Market: A small but delightful array of Jamaican canned and bottled products including canned ackee, callaloo and beans, along with a nice but small selection of preserves. We like their mango chutney and guava jam. linsteadmarketja.com

Matouk's: A Trinidadian brand that makes delicious pepper sauces, jams, chutneys and piccalilli. carolinasauces.com

Pickapeppa Sauce: A must-have for any Jamaican pantry, this is known as the Jamaican steak sauce. It's made from tamarind. pickapeppa.com

Spur Tree: Another well-known brand of jerk seasoning and some preserves, including a nice guava jelly. spurtreejamaica.com

Tastee Patties: Jamaica's number one patty, available frozen for export. tasteejamaica.com

Walkerswood: Best known for their jerk seasoning and sauces. walkerswood.com

INDEX

ACKNOWLEDGEMENTS

This book could never have come to life if not for the efforts, support and guidance of some very special people. We offer sincere gratitude and thanks to the following: our agent Joy Tutela and the David Black Literary Agency for seeing our passion and believing in our dream; our editor Anja Schmidt and Kyle Books for recognising the story of Caribbean people and of our food as worthy of being told; our photographer, Ellen Silverman, for telling the stories of our lives in pictures; our food stylist, Christine Albano, for her clean eye and gifted hands on our recipes; our prop stylist, Marina Malchin, for making every setting have the right balance of sophistication and rusticity that was authentic to our vision; our friend Robyn Moreno for being our guardian angel even when she didn't know it; Uncle Pat for opening the door to the origins of the Rousseau family and how they made their way to Jamaica; Aunt Hester for allowing us to use her beautiful home and gardens; Helen and Aunty Kay for stories of Manga and the Grey/Briggs family; Aunt Cissy and Aunt Nena for their memories and information about the McAllister and Holness sides of the family; our staff, especially Petra, Sandy and Dalton; Hyacinth and Rohan for helping to keep everything in order; Alex and Jonno Edwards and Bromley for giving us a place to write along with great food and company; Rolando Prendagast and Kristal Jackson of Helium Media for their creativity, energy and inspired thinking; Natalia Welsh for coming on board at just the right time and being focused, organised and indispensable in helping us complete the manuscript; Cookie Kinkead for her quick response and the lovely photo of Norma Shirley; the indomitable Pat Ramsay; Jason and Richard Sharp of Cafe Blue and Clifton Mount Estate for their continuing loyalty, friendship and support, and for never saying no; Kyle Mais and Jamaica Inn for generously accommodating us at the last minute in the midst of a very busy day; Ainsley and Marjorie Henriques and Patrick and Marguerite Lynch for being lively and patient dinner guests; Winsome and Crystal Edge for the delicious food and accommodating staff; Brian Meeks for being a great friend; John Lynch and the Jamaica Tourist Board team for their support; Gail Moaney and the Finn Partners team; Jody Staley for her spiritual guidance through thick and thin; our parents Peter and Bev for being supreme testers, tasters and readers; a special thanks to Liam and Jude for keeping us young at heart and for being our biggest fans.